Contents

M000035146

MAXIMUM PRICE ONLY

Andrea Dya

Entertaining Success — 150 ways   2
MAKING IT EASY, TIME SAVERS, FOOD PLANNING,
PARTY THEMES, HOSTESSING TIPS

Pantry Planner   12
WHAT TO HAVE ON HAND

Blooming Ideas   14
INNOVATIVE WAYS WITH FLOWERS AND FOLIAGE

Coping with Kids   26
A NEED-TO-KNOW GUIDE

Become Money Wise   34
A BEGINNER'S GUIDE

Tapping Your Resources   44
MONEY SAVERS AND MONEY SPINNERS

Gardening   52
50 PROBLEM-SOLVERS FOR BUSY PEOPLE

Découpage   64
DECORATING WITH PAPER CUT OUTS

Pizazz with Paint   72
SPATTER, SPONGE, STIPPLE TECHNIQUES, PAPER
STENCILLING

Individual Flair   86
CLEVER DECORATING

Busy Hands   90
THINGS TO MAKE: CROSS STITCH FROG, WALLABY,
QUILT AND CUSHIONS, PAPIER MÂCHÉ, FANTASY
FLOWERS

Cook-and-Wrap!   114
GIFTS TO MAKE IN THE KITCHEN

Christmas Countdown   120
PLAN FOR FUN

Index   127

150 Ways to Entertaining Success
PLANNING MAKES IT EASY

The key to successful entertaining: simple, creative ideas that help you become more confident, efficient and organised. Many people have their own individual style; they tend to specialize in a certain type of party — perhaps last minute get-togethers, do-ahead dinners, casual or elegant occasions. Know your own special style and have fun developing it. Lucy Clayton gives tips on how to organise your recipes, create atmosphere and delegate jobs.

*Successful entertaining is all about food, atmosphere and the trimmings . . . recipes for the delicious desserts and the festive drinks **above**, are on page 128.*

Cocktail parties

There is a big difference between a whopping success and a thudding flop. The secret to a cocktail party's success is to provide interesting drinks, selective music (not too loud) and outgoing people, who are good conversationalists. Food should be memorable.

Points to remember:

● Look after your guests, make them feel special, concentrate on introductions and chat to everyone during the evening. Circulate with a bottle, jug of cocktails or plate of tempting food.

● A serve-yourself drinks table will take some of the load off the host and hostess (especially if you are single) and promote interaction between your friends.

● Do not serve food that is difficult to eat; it is awkward to juggle a glass as well as food.

● Invest in inexpensive glasses (not plastic ones!) for your cocktail parties, or hire them. Beautiful glasses, of course, make your guests feel special.

● For speedy preparation and easy serving, cover a table with an attractive cloth and arrange a hearty display of food: for example, a big basket of assorted breads, a whole ham, a smoked turkey, a well ripened large brie or camembert (Australian brands are excellent). Include an array of mustards and cranberry sauce, plenty of softened butter, several knives, two carving knives and forks and cut-

ting boards for bread and cheese. This may seem expensive, but it is very quick and easy to prepare. Generously scatter bowls of cornchips and avocado dip, nuts and pretzels around the room. Remember lots of ashtrays. No need in this case to hand food around — the hungry ones will congregate around the food table and the rest of the guests will be within arm's reach of a nibbles bowl.

● With more time for advance preparation, many foods may be frozen and simply thawed and reheated eg: fillo triangles, savoury-filled choux puffs, or sausage rolls ready to bake in the oven. Ribbon sandwiches need only be thawed and covered with a damp cloth until ready to serve. Foods that can be made the day before include mini quiches (although pastry shops sell excellent ones).

● Delicatessens offer quick cocktail party foods such as pâtés, terrines, taramasolata, spiced olives, smoked salmon and trout. Make an antipasto platter.

● If mixed drinks or cocktails are served, investigate the cost of hiring a waiter to assist. Or ask a

friend to fill the bill in a dinner suit.

● Have a champagne party — easier and cheaper than you think if you search out good Australian champagne-style wines. Have soft drinks and beer available for non-champagne drinkers. And make bubbles the theme, with pretty balloons. Long, slim glasses, tapering from rim to a narrow base are designed to display and sustain the golden effervescence.

● Punch parties are popular and easy; concoct a lively and decorative alcoholic punch to last the whole evening.

● Serve substantial food if you expect the party to continue beyond the traditional cocktail hours. Plan to serve 10 different items, five cold and five hot. A good mix would be ribbon sandwiches, prawns dipped in avocado sauce, cubes of roast beef topped with saté sauce, vegetable crudites dipped in mayonnaise, oysters, mini quiches, chicken drumsticks, felafel dipped in hummus, chippolata sausages dipped in tomato relish, sausage rolls with tomato sauce. Supply cocktail toothpicks and small paper napkins for guests.

penne

macaroni

fettucine....

tortellini

spaghetti

pieces, small whole trout, bream or snapper, or little racks of lamb.

● Serve only two vegetables or a simple salad with a potato dish.

● Consider featuring one or two courses at home, then going out for dessert and coffee.

● Substitute dessert with a healthy fruit platter, eaten with fingers, served with coffee and chocolates (saves washing up too).

● Provide a fun start by handing each guest a party cocktail as they arrive — choose a popular one such as a banana daiquiri, pina colada, marguerita or peach fizz.

How to open a champagne bottle: remove metal foil carefully; hold cork firmly while removing the wire hood. Point bottle away from you and your guests at a 45 degree angle. Hold cork with one hand, grasp the bottle firmly in your other hand by the neck of the body. Twist the bottle one quarter turn in each direction — the cork should begin to ease out. If not, repeat the movement steadily, a quarter turn at a time. Exert counter pressure as the cork pops out. Do not let cork fly!

Dinner parties

For busy people, dinner party entertaining is made easy with the ability to prepare everything at short notice, or to be organised ahead and prepare most of the food in advance:

● For a no-time-to-cook dinner party, perhaps on a week night, serve only two courses (eating light is the rule these days). Choose between an entree or dessert. Serve coffee with chocolates if no dessert is served, otherwise serve coffee with dessert.

● Settle upon serve-at-the-table dishes. This saves washing up and allows you to spend more time with your friends.

● Fresh pasta is a favourite and readily available in city centres. Make a quick cream sauce, add bacon and mushrooms or seafood.

● Fresh asparagus with a processor-made Hollandaise sauce makes a quick, delicious entree.

● Make a quick sauce to serve over icecream or serve fresh berries with a liqueur-flavoured whipped cream.

● To save washing up, serve the entree, perhaps pâté or prettily arranged, interesting cheeses, as a substantial hors d'oeuvre with pre-dinner drinks.

● Keep salads simple (for entrees or as an accompaniment): one kind of lettuce, avocado, bacon or toasted pecans and a French dressing. A lovely light and healthy way to start a meal.

● Choose cuts of meat or fish that need little preparation such as fillets of any kind (beef, pork, chicken, fish, lamb or veal) chicken

Cook-ahead, no-fuss ideas

● Soups make a satisfying entree with fresh bread and butter. They are inexpensive and can be frozen or made a couple of days ahead. Popular are pumpkin, carrot, spinach, pea and lettuce, mushroom, French onion — the list is endless.

● Pasta with made-ahead sauce is terrific as a main course or a substantial entree. Make a rich tomato sauce ahead; add seafood when reheating the sauce.

● Main course dishes prepared ahead and frozen, or baked and ready to reheat, or just prepared ready for final baking are ideal. Possibilities include lasagna, moussaka, veal parmagiana or chicken pieces in a sauce. Casseroles are always appreciated.

● If serving rice, cook ahead and reheat over a steamer or in the microwave for a few minutes.

● By the time dessert is served, the hostess will greatly appreciate one that has been made ahead — anything from the simplest poached pear to an elaborate torte.

● Homemade icecreams (that are more like frozen mousses) make a very quick and easy dessert that can be prepared the morning of the party or the day before. Make with 4 eggs beaten with 1 cup sugar, fold in a 300ml carton whipped cream and add your favourite flavour (perhaps fresh passionfruit, melted chocolate, raisins soaked in rum); pour into a shallow loaf pan, freeze several hours or until set. Serve straight from the freezer with a crunchy wafer biscuit.

Buffets

Ideal for the solo hostess.

● Two types: sit down, or stand up, with fork food.

● Choose dishes that can be served either cold or at room temperature.

● Limit number of hot dishes but have large amounts of each.

● Butter bread or rolls.

● For a crowd — set out buffet with identical foods on both sides of the table so that two lines form.

● Allow room beside dishes for guests to put their plates down and easily serve themselves; this is important for salads.

● Have plates at the beginning and place utensils wrapped in napkins at the end of the buffet line.

● Have a collection of trays handy for anyone who may have difficulty balancing a plate.

● Keep buffet table looking neat — make sure it is free of empty and half-empty glasses.

● Create a warm atmosphere with lots of candles, but be careful not to clutter the buffet table with them and obscure dishes.

● Use colourful sheets or even light bedspreads if you run out of tablecloths.

● Serve coffee with a large basket of assorted biscuits, slices and little cakes or tartlets rather than dessert (again less washing up.)

● If serving carved hot or cold meat such as ham or roast beef at a sit down buffet, have someone carve at the buffet table as the meat is required. Have someone assisting the serving of dishes to

speed up the buffet line.

● Cold seafood buffets can be prepared ahead. Serve a whole poached fish with skin removed, prawns, oysters, mussels on the half shell, Tahitian fish salad, sashimi, crabs and lobsters for extravagant occasions. Provide ample numbers of finger bowls and salads, bread, butter and mayonnaise of differing flavours.

● Cold summer buffets with hams, cold meats, salads and bread make entertaining easy on the night. Make them seem more elaborate by providing serviettes of vivid colours, small bowls of flowers, a cornucopia of fresh fruits.

Brunch and breakfast parties

● Stand-up champagne breakfasts with a 10am start are ideal for about 20 people. Serve hot savoury-filled croissants and paper napkins. Fillings of leg ham and tasty cheese, or combinations of chicken, mushroom and sour cream filling are good choices.

● Sit-down breakfasts for eight, 10 or 12 guests are surprisingly easy if you serve croissants, whipped cream and jam and a platter of sliced fruit followed by (if they are still hungry) a scrambled egg dish with hot toast waiting in the oven. Make the scrambled egg interesting by flavouring it with smoked salmon and dill or sauteed mushrooms and shallots. Allow two to three eggs for each person; and for variation, use cream or sour cream instead of milk.

Novelty party ideas

● Clear your living room floor and serve a Middle Eastern or Indian feast or Chinese hot pot (or steamboat) on an authentic, colourful cloth or mats with lots of cushions. Takeaway dishes may help to supplement some or all of the dishes as a time-saver. Other possible food themes: Japanese, Mexican, Greek. Or have a South East Asian feast and provide a medley of dishes from Thai, Korean, Malaysian, Indonesian and Indian takeaway restaurants.

● Themes always add more fun to a party — St Patrick's Day inspires thoughts of green food and decor.

● Games nights are fun for casual entertaining — cards, Trivial Pursuit, backgammon tournaments or monopoly. Serve hot soup in mugs and sandwiches or jaffles.

● Intrigue with a masked party.

St Patrick's Day

Celebrate March 17 with a green theme. Here, some suggestions to inspire unusual menus:

Cream of Spinach Soup

Chicken Fillets with Basil Hollandaise
Baby New Potatoes with Parsley Butter
Steamed Broccoli with Lemon

Vanilla Icecream with Creme de Menthe Sauce

Green and White Pasta with Zucchini

Fish Fillets with Basil Hollandaise
Baby New Potatoes with Chive Butter
Green Salad

Chocolate Cake with Creme de Menthe Cream

● Quiches are quick once you perfect a basic formula. For preference have shortcrust pastry made and frozen or use pre-rolled pastry; otherwise make it quickly with the processor or use fillo pastry or breadcrumbs as a quick base. Use a 26cm quiche dish with two cups of filling (for example, spinach, mushroom, salmon or bacon and broccoli), 4 eggs and a 300ml carton of thickened cream, some grated cheese and season to taste, then bake in a moderate oven for 40 minutes or until set.

● A pleasant touch is to have extra copies of the Sunday or Saturday paper for a relaxed breakfast party; although reading should not be encouraged for the full party period!

miso soup, noodles, tofu...

Christmas in June

Many people who've moved here from Europe or North America hold mid-winter Christmas parties. The aromatic beckonings of golden roast turkey, plum pudding, seasonings, lovely winter vegetables are so much more rewarding when the weather is cold.

Cold weather also makes Santa Claus seem more authentic and rich plum puddings with lashings of custard easier to consume.

Roast pork is a good alternative 'Christmas' offering in June — rub the skin with lemon before cooking to get a really good crackling. As a last resort, you can finish off a not-so-crisp crackling under the griller.

Time-saving tips

- Group similar preparation methods together, eg, wash all vegetables in the sink together.
- If you need onion for more than one recipe, chop it all at once.
- Decide what can be made ahead and frozen or make a day or two before. Many dishes even taste better made ahead.
- Grate cheese in the processor and store it in the refrigerator.
- Make and freeze breadcrumbs in ready-to-use one cup bags.
- Freeze stock in icecube trays and one cup containers for sauces.
- Crush unpeeled garlic cloves in the garlic crusher.
- Chop vegetables in bundles, such as beans and shallots.
- Use dry measuring cups over again without washing, just shake excess out.
- Use your microwave as a time-saving appliance to:
1. Soften butter on High for about 30 seconds.
2. Melt butter on High one minute.
3. Melt chopped chocolate on High 30 seconds.
4. Dissolve gelatine in cold water on High 30 seconds.
5. Reheat cooked rice, casseroles and soups.
6. Cook bacon placed between paper towels.
7. Blanch and steam vegetables.
8. Steam fish.
- The food processor is a versatile and time-saving appliance. Use to:
1. Puree soups, sauces and pate.
2. Make savoury butters.
3. Make mayonnaise and hollandaise sauce.
4. Chop onions, bacon, ham, nuts, herbs, meats.
5. Crush biscuits.
6. Make breadcrumbs.
7. Slice celery and mushrooms.
8. Grate cheese, carrots, zucchini and potatoes.
- To peel tomatoes — hold tomato over gas flame with a fork or place in bowl and pour boiling water over, stand 30 seconds.
- Cut jacket potatoes in half lengthways to bake in half the time.
- Chop canned tomatoes in the can with kitchen scissors or a sharp knife.
- Roll an orange, lemon or lime on a hard surface before squeezing, to get the most juice out of them.
- Use your wok frequently.

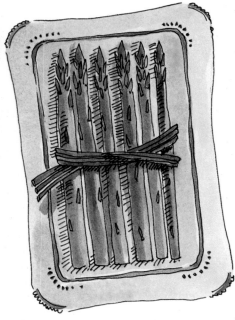

Quantities

It is often difficult to judge how much people will eat. No one wants too many leftovers unless they have organised to cook for another meal at the same time.
- Extra rice, pasta or potatoes can always be used in another meal the next day — make a main course salad or a hearty casserole or soup. Extra rice freezes well.
- Soggy salad is not very good the next day. You could serve the dressing separately at the table so that any leftover salad can be used the next day. This is a good idea for holiday cooking. Allow about half a cup of dressing for a salad to serve six people.
- Allow one-third cup raw rice per person, more if it is a buffet.
- Allow 100g dried pasta per person for a main course serving, less for an entree.
- Allow 125g baby new potatoes per person or one medium whole potato; cook a few extra.
- Work out the amount of vegetable accompaniments at the fruit and vegetable market. It will depend on how many vegetables you are serving. Count out handfuls of vegetables for the number of guests — a good method for beans, snow peas, baby mushrooms, baby squash and new potatoes. If you think about it at the shop you can usually guess how much you will need. A little thought can prevent you buying too much or worse, not enough.

Kitchen sense

Many factors contribute to kitchen organisation — time planning and checklists, efficient preparation and menu planning, do-ahead work and efficient shopping lists:
- Have a time plan — in your head, written out in full or just a quick list. Make sure you have the time to do everything — if you don't, get someone to help you or cut something out — simplify the menu.
- Co-ordinate dishes to use the oven, hot plates and microwave and cold dishes that need refrigeration and freezer space.
- Keep last minute cooking to an absolute minimum.
- Make a checklist in order of what can be done two days before, one day before, morning of party and several hours before and last minute — cross each job off the list as you go.
- Remember to delegate wherever possible.
- Remember to include jobs on your list like:
1. Coffee tray.
2. Bathroom.
3. Waste paper baskets.
4. Drinks.
5. Front hall or path.
6. Serving dishes and plates.
7. Cookware.
- Clean up as much as you can as you go — while you are cooking, rinse plates and serving dishes, stack dishwasher if you have one, refrigerate leftovers.
- Make an organised shopping list. Don't assume you can remember how much you have left of a certain ingredient — check it! Check off everything you need from your recipes.
- Separate your shopping list into sections for supermarket, fruit and vegetables, butcher, delicatessen, cheese shop and bottle shop.
- If you know your supermarket well (and fruit and vegetable market), list the ingredients in the order they appear in the aisles.

- **Use your tastebuds when cooking to check the flavour.**
- **Develop your confidence with the flavour and texture of food.**
- **Just use a teaspoon to sample a small amount. You don't need to consume a lot.**

Picnics

Use this checklist before every picnic to avoid the disaster of forgetting a vital ingredient!

1. Corkscrew and bottle opener.
2. Rugs, table cloth
3. Unbreakable plates, glasses and mugs.
4. Knives, forks, salad servers, tongs.
5. Napkins, paper towels, tissues.
6. Icebox.
7. Vacuum flask.
8. Pepper grinder, salt.
9. Fire lighting equipment — paper, matches, charcoal.
10. Serrated knife and cutting board.
11. Butter.
12. Plastic garbage bags.
13. Insect repellent and sunscreen.
14. Milk and sugar.

● Picnics are ideal for those without a garden.

● Plan for a minimum of preparation at the picnic site — have meats sliced or in individual pieces, salads made ready to serve, and the bread already buttered.

● Consider a hot winter picnic with hot chicken drumsticks, foil wrapped jacket potatoes and a warm vegetable salad. Keep food warm with foil. Take rugs and old cushions. Warm up with a ball game and soak up the winter sun.

● Slices and biscuits are easy for something sweet with coffee rather than a messy dessert.

● Picnics are informal enough for you to ask other people to contribute food; it allows busy mothers to share the workload around.

● Late afternoon and night picnics are just as enjoyable as those at lunchtime, especially with daylight saving. Start around 6pm and watch the sunset.

● Have a spontaneous picnic — just stop at the delicatessen, fruit shop and bottle shop and get all the supplies you need. Your lunch hour and a convenient park are excuse enough to go alfresco.

Barbecues

Barbecues are the great Australian way of celebrating our informal lifestyles. The advantages:

1. Men get more involved with the cooking.
2. Less mess is made in the kitchen from cooking.
3. Foods taste wonderful cooked on the barbecue.
4. Menus tend to be simple.
5. Guests are relaxed and informal.
6. They are ideal for beach, caravan or camping holidays.

● Some foods are better if they are precooked in the oven, eg, chicken pieces, because they tend to dry out and burn easily on the barbecue. Finish cooking them on the barbecue for about 10-15 minutes to allow the barbecue flavour to penetrate. Food prepared and cooked the day before saves time in the morning.

● Olive oil in marinades prevents meat sticking to the barbecue. Brush oil on meat before cooking if no marinade is used.

- Serve barbecued prawns in the shell, spare ribs or chicken wings as an entree, eaten with the fingers. Supply enough finger bowls and napkins for guests (saves washing up entree plates).
- A cold entree at a barbecue could be fresh prawns served on a tray lined with crushed ice (make ice with water dyed blue with food colouring). Again, have plenty of finger bowls.
- Hot ratatouille and warm salads in winter are a great alternative to cold salads at a barbecue.
- For outdoor eating it is worth investing in a couple of bright and cheery umbrellas for both atmosphere and comfort.
- Evening barbecues are romantic and exotic on hot summer nights. Hurricane lamps and flares create atmospheric lighting. Burn mosquito coils or use mosquito repellent.

Afternoon teas

- In these days of lighter eating, an afternoon business meeting can be just as successful as a business lunch or dinner.
- Afternoon teas can celebrate a graduation, an engagement or even a wedding — and they need not apply only to women.
- Afternoon games of croquet or Trivial Pursuit or more energetic tennis matches are ideal for serving afternoon tea.
- Ribbon sandwiches, made ahead and frozen, thaw quickly.
- Little cakes, tartlets, slices and biscuits may be bought or made ahead and frozen.
- Make a fresh jug of lemonade as a sweet, old-fashioned touch. See recipe at right.
- Don't forget the tea — good old Billy tea is terrific outdoors.
- No alcohol need be served (a money-saver).

Hostessing

The first impression you make on your guests will set the tone for the rest of the party.

Set a welcoming impression by:
1. Being dressed and ready when the first guest arrives.
2. Having the aroma of something in the hallway — lovely cooking smells, or fresh flowers or potpourris or even your own perfume (spray some in the hallway).
3. Having music playing.
4. Having relaxed lighting.
5. Having drinks ready to pour or quickly encouraging guests to help themselves.
6. Making clear introductions — they are important. Try to use everybody's full name and introduce something special about them, for example, good sailor, guitar player, or just a terrific person.
7. Making your guests feel at home by walking with them to the area where you are entertaining.
8. Appearing relaxed. If you seem tense, your guests will feel tense. Try to relax a little before they arrive, even if it only means sitting down for five minutes and taking a few deep breaths.

If you have a disaster in the kitchen, the best way to handle it is to laugh it off with an amusing comment. Your guests will feel uncomfortable if they see that you are upset. You can maintain your equilibrium in the face of any disaster, there is always takeaway if you are desperate or even a restaurant. People remember your charm as a hostess far longer than they do your cooking abilities.

- Invite no more people than you can cope with — decide how many can fit at the table or in your backyard or how many you can serve; are there enough plates, glasses and chairs?
- Cook recipes you have made before and feel confident with.
- When you invite people, give a specific time to arrive and the type of party — it gives people an idea of the dress and mood to expect.
- It's a good idea to ask people about food allergies and dislikes.
- Don't hesitate to invite an extra male or female guest.
- Eat on time, rather than spoil the meal. If anyone is very late, ring them and start without them.

Atmosphere

- Atmosphere is created by your choice of lighting, music, table settings, decorations and the clever use of space. The right mix makes a party a memorable occasion.
- Lamp lighting, lights with dimmer switches and track lighting are gentler than overhead lights, which tend to create a harsh glare. Try candlelight for subtlety and a touch of romance.
- Music soothes the soul, breaks the ice and helps people relax and enjoy themselves. Music can also create an atmosphere for a special theme — anything from a romantic dinner for two to a boisterous Greek-style dinner party.
- Tablesettings of beautiful silver, table linen, china dinner sets and crystal glasses help create elegance but they are not essential. If you haven't enough matching table settings, mix and match a lively collection of place mats, table napkins, dinner plates or glasses to create a setting with plenty of colour and character. Colourful

> **LEMONADE**
> **The best way to make lemonade is the old fashioned way with fresh lemon juice, sweetened and diluted. Use ½ cup sugar dissolved in 1½ litres water and add ½ cup lemon juice.**

Instead of spending $20 on flowers for a centrepiece, invest in small terracotta pots (these cost $10) into which you can pop pretty flowers in season.

side plates enhance plain coloured dinner plates. Unusual soup bowls of differing patterns add interest and individuality.

● Fresh flowers enliven every room. Put them in the hallway, on the dinner table, in the living room, bathroom and room where guests will leave their jackets. On the dinner table have a low arrangement of flowers or foliage so that the conversation is not disrupted — don't create any sort of barrier.

● The dinner or buffet table can be decorated with bowls of fresh herbs in white vases — use mint, parsley or basil. A rustic array of nuts in the shell with pretty seeds and pine cones, collected in your travels, arranged in a little basket, look lovely. A bowl of shiny red apples, tomatoes or other sparkling fresh fruit or vegetables can create a magnificent still life.

● Other ornaments (for example, a favourite wooden duck) in the centre of the table between two candlesticks can substitute for fresh flowers.

● Create a cosy sense of space when you entertain. Dining rooms need to feel intimate but not cramped and stifling.

● Round tables are suitable for four to eight people; any more and the distance is too great. Rectangular tables can be longer but it is better if they are narrow, with just enough room for the place settings. Intimacy is created when people are close together, without being cramped.

● Check the room temperature. Remember that you will feel hotter because you have been cooking but often guests can be uncomfortably cold without you knowing.

Be prepared

● Having certain stand-bys on hand makes entertaining easier, cuts down shopping and helps in emergencies.

● Make batches of tomato sauce, meat sauce and stock and freeze them — great to have on hand for a last minute pasta dish or soup.

● Always have a ready supply of condiments you use regularly such as mustards, cranberry sauce, red currant and mint jellies to use in sauces and gravies; jams, marmalades and long-life milk and cream for impromptu afternoon teas; mayonnaise, chutneys, pickles, olives, dry biscuits, capers, ready-made salad dressing for spontaneous lunches; unground coffee beans and eggs will always come in handy for last minute guests.

● Grow herbs in pots or in the garden — basil in summer, mint, parsley and chives all year round.

● Keep in your freezer — bacon, some meat, chicken, fish, pastry, peas, and icecream.

● If you can live with the temptation, also have chocolates and sweets to serve with coffee, cornchips, and other nibbles to serve with drinks.

● Keep cans of tomatoes, salmon,

asparagus, corn, tuna, smoked oysters, camembert and brie cheeses, soup, fruit and peppers.

● Keep your linen cupboard ship-shape to avoid last minute hassles. Keep items on hand that you use all the time, for example, both formal and informal placemats, tablecloths, table runners and table napkins; paper napkins, cocktail toothpicks, doilies, candlesticks with wax catchers and fresh candles, place cards and holders.

Delegating

● Capture as much help as you can from husband and children. Jobs to delegate are:

1. Table setting.

2. Check bathroom, puff up cushions, dust, sweep, wash up.

3. Pass around the hors d'oeuvres.

4. Toss salads.

5. Barbecue food.

6. Serving the courses: put sauce in a jug, bread into basket, vegetables on plates.

7. Clear tables, rinse dishes.

8. Make and serve coffee.

9. Refill drinks.

10. Wash up.

● If hiring staff make a list and run through it with them before guests arrive to avoid misunderstandings.

Pantry Planner
WHAT TO HAVE ON HAND

In the refrigerator

- Milk
- Butter
- Margarine
- Eggs (use for making soufflés, crêpes, omelettes)
- Fresh cream (use in sauces and over desserts)
- Sour cream (ideal in sauces)
- Yoghurt, plain (use in salad dressings; as a dessert with a variety of fruits)
- Cheddar cheese
- Parmesan in a piece (use freshly grated over pasta dishes)
- Bacon
- Frankfurts
- Joint of cooked ham (keep wrapped in a damp tea-towel to ensure ham stays moist and does not become salty; a pillow case is ideal to ensure that it is completely covered. Do not wrap in plastic wrap or ham will become slimey)
- Nuts, various (raw cashews and almonds are a useful addition to salads or Asian recipes; pine-nuts added to a stuffing for poultry add excitement)
- Salad dressing (home-made or commercial brand)
- Mayonnaise
- Olives, gherkins, capers, green peppercorns (chop up finely and add to sauces and to salads)

In the freezer

- Peas, beans, mixed vegetables, corn kernels, spinach
- Icecream (serve with fresh fruit or fruit purées for dessert)
- Puff and fillo pastry (cut down on the preparation time for sweet and savoury pies and flans)
- Puréed unsweetened raspberries (delicious served as a topping for icecream)
- Bread (thaws quickly)

In the store-cupboard

- Olive oil for salad dressings and some pan-fried dishes
- A good, all-purpose cooking oil
- A good range of dried herbs and spices such as mixed herbs, tarragon, oregano, cayenne, curry powder, cumin, cardamom, paprika, nutmeg, cinnamon, cloves (can store for six months before they become stale)
- Black peppercorns, ground white pepper
- Table salt and rock salt
- Soy sauce (adds an Oriental flavour to stir-fried vegetables, meats and poultry)
- Worcestershire sauce
- Mint sauce and jelly
- Chicken and beef stock cubes (for flavour in casseroles)
- Garlic paste in a tube or jar (once opened, wrap securely and store in the refrigerator)
- Tomato sauce
- Dry mustard and a ready-made mustard (as accompaniments to cold meats, in salad dressings and sauces)
- Golden breadcrumbs (as coatings for fish and poultry which is to be pan-fried)
- Gelatine (for setting sweet and savoury mousses)
- Various flavours of jelly crystals
- Junket tablets
- Dried yeast (use when making your own bread. Freeze loaves not required immediately)
- Plain and self-raising flour (once opened, store in airtight containers or in the refrigerator, to avoid insect infestation)
- Cornflour (store as above; use for sauces, custards, baking)
- Bicarbonate of soda
- Baking powder
- Castor and brown sugar
- Icing sugar
- Cooking chocolate
- Vanilla essence (add to chocolate desserts, custards, cakes)

- Evaporated milk in tins, tubes or cartons
- Marmalade, jam, honey
- Vegemite, peanut butter
- Breakfast cereals, oats, wheatgerm (use oats for making flapjacks; coat slices of liver in wheatgerm and pan-fry)
- White and brown rice, short-grain rice for puddings
- Pasta, various shapes, colours, sizes, flavours
- Wine vinegar (use for dressings and sauces)
- Tins of tuna, sardines, salmon, crab, prawns and anchovies (can be used as a base for mousses, to stuff avocadoes, to accompany simple dishes)
- Tins of whole, peeled tomatoes, artichoke hearts, potatoes, corn kernels (tomatoes make a good sauce for pasta dishes; artichoke hearts served with slices of salami and olives make a quick hors d'oeuvre; potatoes can be used in salads or simply heated as a vegetable accompaniment, slathered in butter with chopped herbs; corn kernels make a good base for a chowder or soup)
- Dried pulses such as red kidney beans and lentils (soak overnight and add to casseroles or cook and serve as an accompaniment to vegetables
- Dried mushrooms (more useful than tinned as you only need to use a few at a time to add great flavour to risottos, stir-fried dishes and sauces). Soak a few mushrooms in warm water for an hour, slice and use as required. Keep packet sealed to maintain their quality
- Dried fruits such as apples, apricots, prunes, sultanas, raisins (soak overnight and use as a dessert or as an accompaniment to some meat dishes. Store in the refrigerator once packets are opened as dried foodstuffs are subject to insect infestation)
- Canned fruits such as apricots, pineapple rings, cherries (can be

Being pressed for time is one of life's most common stresses. A job to cope with and a family to look after can make cooking just one more chore to slot into a busy lifestyle. Much of the anxiety of meal preparation can be avoided if you maintain a strategically-stocked pantry — it will be a money and a time saver. We give a list of items to have on hand so that you always have the ingredients to make interesting, quick meals. Plus ideas to help make cooking a pleasure rather than an obligation.

baked with different toppings or puréed and served as a sauce)
● A variety of canned and packet soups (good as a base to a stew)
● Instant coffee, tea, cocoa

In a cool, dry place

● Potatoes
● Onions
● Garlic

In the fruit bowl

● Apples, oranges, bananas (never mix together as apples speed up the ripening process)
● Seasonal soft fruits kept in the refrigerator will last several days

In the drink cupboard

● White and red wine (add flavour to sauces)
● Grand Marnier (macerate fresh fruit such as oranges in Grand Marnier for an hour or so, for a simple dessert)
● Port (use in sauces)
● Sherry (use in Oriental recipes)

Useful checklist

● Handy utensils to have for quick cooking are a wok (ideal for stir-frying), a steamer (retains nutrients), a mouli-sieve (quickly purées vegetables and fruit). Cut down on pots and pans whenever possible. A double steamer will take care of the vegetables and the meat or fish all at the same time. Cook fish in a package of foil, with butter and lemon, in the oven. All the goodness is retained and there's no washing up.
● When making items such as pastry, cakes, crêpes, casseroles, sauce for spaghetti, make a double quantity and freeze.

● When you're in a hurry, buy fresh pasta rather than dried. It will cook in boiling water in about three to five minutes.
● Grow your own parsley, mint and chives — in pots on the window sill if you live in a flat. Plant a lemon tree for virtually a year-round supply of lemons.
● Remember that a dash of wine from the cask or a slug of port will cheer up a basic sauce.
● Don't just use the barbecue for weekend entertaining. Buy ready-to-cook kebabs (available from good butchers) or make your own.
● Draw up a list of 10 tried and tested recipes which you know you can put together with store-cupboard items in 15 minutes with a maximum of 30 minutes cooking time. Rotate these old faithfuls regularly.
● As soon as you open a new packet or tin, write it on your shopping list. (One of those wipe-down boards you can hang in your kitchen is best.) Buying everything on the list at your weekly or fortnightly shopping expedition will cut down the risk of running out of anything.
● Buy large quantities where possible: large cans or bottles of cooking oil, tomato sauce, fruit juices, for instance (do the same with washing powders and toiletries). This is a far more economical way to buy.
● Pay attention to the use-by dates now featured on many foodstuffs. Always throw out any food which has a strange smell, cold meats which have become slimey, even if the use-by date has not been reached.
● Check if some tinned foods need to be stored in the refrigerator — there will be instructions on the side of the can. Once a tin of food is opened, keep contents in the refrigerator and be sure to use them within a couple of days.

Put contents in glass or plastic container to store them.
● Foods with strong odours such as seafood and some cheeses must be wrapped in the refrigerator. Do not store them near milk, cream or yoghurt as they may taint the dairy products.
● The upper shelves of the refrigerator are the coldest part — store items there that you want to keep the longest or which are likely to spoil quickly eg: seafood, chicken and cheeses.
● Uncooked poultry and fish should not be kept longer than two days at around 2°C. Keep meat for a maximum of five days, preferably shorter and milk for five. Cheese and butter will survive happily for over a month, but, obviously, the fresher they are, the better.
● When storing bottles of fruit juices in the refrigerator after initial opening, squeeze container slightly to expel air prior to tightening the cap. This creates negative air pressure inside the container, preventing drips.
● After pan-frying meat or poultry, de-glaze the pan by adding a dash of port, white wine or stock. Reduce the liquid by about a third, scraping up the juices and delicious crusty bits left by the meat and stirring them in. Add butter if you wish and pour sauce over the meat or poultry.
● If possible, make your own stock (chicken, beef or fish) and freeze in 300 ml quantities.
● Look out for leaflets in your local butcher's, fish shop and vegetable shop advising on new cuts of meat, newly available fruits. Recipes are also often provided which lay great emphasis on quick-to-prepare food. Contact your local branch of the Department of Agriculture, Fish Marketing Authority or the CSIRO if you have problems regarding finding the ingredients you want and learning how to prepare them.

Blooming Ideas

INNOVATIVE WAYS WITH FLOWERS & FOLIAGE

Flowers can be your greatest decorative asset, as can plant material of all kinds. Friends are coming to dinner, your planned menu includes your greatest successes, wines are organised — but what about the flowers? The garden is bare and you don't have a decent vase? It's surprising what clever hands and unusual ideas can achieve. Don't stick to the traditional ways of flower arrangement; your garden may contain undiscovered treasures. Floral designers Janet Bourke and Nelson Pringle present clever ideas for using flowers (fresh and dried), herbs, leaves and grasses to dress up a dinner party, give a special touch to gifts (see page 120) or provide colour and interest for your home.

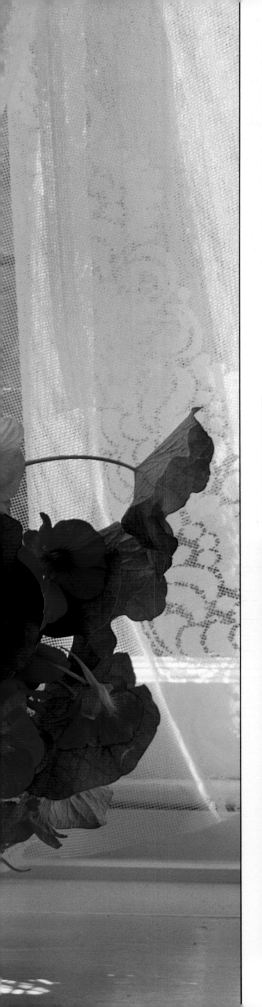

Materials: a good pair of secateurs and scissors; chicken wire (about three metres) from local hardware shop; dry foam block (Oasis), you can buy it by the "brick" at your local florist (don't try to use it again and again; acids from flowers and foliages build up in the block and will reduce the life of your next arrangement. Always soak the dry foam block for at least half an hour before using in a container); a roll of adhesive tape; plastic garbage bags; floristry wire (available from florist suppliers). These are your basic tools; we will add to the list of mechanics as we demonstrate each idea. Always keep your containers clean, wash out with hot water and detergent after use.

A tip for glassware, particularly if the shape is difficult to clean: fill the container with warm water and drop a couple of Steradent tablets into the water and leave. You will be amazed at what comes off; even try it on that port-stained decanter!

Cone of flowers

Nasturtiums are abundant and can be simple to use as decoration. Picked in a bunch and placed in a glass bowl this easily grown flower delights the eye with vibrant colour. Or add unexpected style and elegance with the technique below.

Place a full brick of soaked foam

block upright in a container and shave into a cone shape. Cut a piece of chicken wire and wrap around the cone-shaped foam block. Pick your nasturtiums approximately the same length and gently push the stems into the cone. Cover the wire and cone with shorter nasturtium leaves after the flowers are in place.

Before taking a tour of your garden or ransacking your cupboards, there are a few items you will need to achieve the results you want. Open your cupboards and see what's there. The added bonus of finding vases this way is that your collection will be original. Your containers can be grouped or used by themselves on sideboards, hallstands, bedroom sidetables, in the kitchen, anywhere there is an area you think needs a lift.

Inspect your garden and look at what really is there. The foliage is probably not all one shade of green — sage, emerald, pale and mid green, silver, lime — plus prunus reds, pods, dried heads of flowers and sculpture in a branch of a tree. Take courage and pick only one stem of an annual if that's all there is. You can use it with other ''one's'' and ''two's'' and mixed foliage. Look for colour and texture to complement your vase. Have a peek at your herb garden. Parsley, chives and rosemary can go in the pot and on the table!

If you have containers such as jugs and teapots to substitute for vases, or silver that you don't want water-marked, cut a garbage bin bag to size and line your container with the plastic. Then place a piece of soaked foam block into plastic before you place your flowers. When the flowers have died, remove the bag and foam block and your container remains unmarked.

To prevent the flowers from spilling out of a shallow but wide-topped bowl while trying to arrange them, dry the container well and make a grid with adhesive tape across the top of the container. Work your flowers in sections and you will find each grid will support the stems. For a smaller container, use a piece of chicken wire over the top of the rim. Secure it with string or floristry wire and use the holes in the wire as support for the stems.

When your garden doesn't have blooms, but your lemon tree has fruit: cut a spray of foliage, pick your lemons and attach bows of ribbon to fruit with a pin and run a ribbon streamer to the base of the spray for a centrepiece.

Top tables

Formally festive, indoor, outdoor, or casual, dress your table to suit the occasion.

We used a soup bowl as our container, placed a piece of soaked foam block into the bowl and covered it with chicken wire; this prevents the foam block breaking up when the stems go in. Cut the wire at the centre in which to place a candle; the foam block acts as the candle holder. Now fill the bowl with different coloured and textured foliage.

To make a special occasion even prettier, place a "gift" of flowers on each napkin and tie with two or three fine ribbons in matching tonings.

Basket of flowers

To achieve our basket collage: fill a basket with small containers (even the humble jam jar), and place groups of flowers and foliage in each container. Don't mix your flowers too much, keep them grouped as shown. This will avoid a "spotted" look. If the containers are showing above the rim of the basket, gather some ivy and wrap the inside edge of the basket to hide the various containers.

Potpourri

For about the volume of 40 roses, or roses and mixed flowers, have:

10g oil of lavender
2 cinnamon sticks
20g whole cloves
20g ground nutmeg
20g coriander seed
100g orris root powder
100g salt

Gather your roses or mixed flowers making sure they are free of moisture and hang them in a cool, airy place to prevent moulding whilst drying. The laundry is a good spot. When the petals are paper dry put them into an airtight pottery or glass container. For each handful of dried petals, allow a smaller handful of salt.

Place lid on container and leave, stirring twice a day for five days. During this five day period, pick a variety of scented leaves and flowers, such as lavender, rosemary flowers, carnations, scented geranium leaves, bay leaves, lemon-scented verbena, eau-de-cologne mint, orange blossom, violets, wallflowers and jasmine. Dry these on sheets of paper, turning them regularly. On the fifth day, add these to the roses or roses and mixed flowers and salt.

Place some of the orris powder in a cup and add the oil, mix until the consistency is no longer moist but powdery. Add your spices. Small quantities of orange or lemon peel, with all the pith removed, may also be added.

Mix all ingredients together and cover for three or four weeks. Stir potpourri occasionally and enjoy the aroma. If the potpourri becomes too dry, add more salt; if moisture is building up, add more orris root (from health food shops).

Natives

Go native, as pictured above. Collect wattle, the wonderful blossom that is out when little else is. Pick a variety of easy-to-grow grevilleas. You will have to buy waratah and kangaroo paw unless you grow your own, as it is protected. Both do last well in a vase. Give Australiana pride of place. Experiment.

Buy some terracotta pots with saucers and keep them as containers for rosemary, parsley and chives, some seed pods, a bunch of daisies, and pop them on a shelf or window ledge.

Hydrangea cone

Materials: dry foam block (Oasis), chicken wire, plant pot, piece of branch or pole, dried hydrangeas and delphiniums, wire.

1. Put block of foam into pot. Position branch in foam block.

2. Wrap chicken wire around other foam blocks to form a cone shape. Push cone onto branch.

3. Take hydrangea heads apart. Place dried flowers into foam block, leaving a path for delphiniums or other flowers you may wish to include in the design. If flowers' stems are not long enough, attach a piece of wire to them and then push into foam block.

4. Continue with flowers until foam and wire shape is completely covered. Tree can be kept indefinitely.

Spiced wreath

Traditionally, a wreath is hung on the front door at Christmas, but why not make a wreath of herbs and spices to hang in the kitchen all year round?

Materials: wreath base of willow, tied and loosely woven into round shape and left to dry; 22 gauge floristry wire; muslin; ribbons; cinnamon sticks; selection of aromatic spices: cloves, nutmeg, pepper corns; jacaranda pods; fresh rosemary sprigs.

1. Cut your muslin into rounds and fill with a selection of spices, secure with wire. Leave the wires long on all components as these will be used to attach the muslin bags to the wreath base.

2. Cover the wire around the top with ribbons.

3. Place a couple of cinnamon sticks together, wire to secure them and then add ribbon.

4. Individually wire the jacaranda pods. To do this, run the wire across the base of the open pod and secure at the base of the pod where the stem is attached.

5. Cut and wire together small bunches of rosemary sprigs.

6. Now work out your placement, secure pods, sprigs, muslin bags and cinnamon sticks by running your wires through the willow directly under desired position.

7. Secure firmly and cut wires.

8. Bend wire twists back into the willow so that they won't scratch the surface you hang it on or catch when handling. There is no need to make a hanger for the wreath as the open weave of the willow easily hangs on a nail.

Take your spice wreath off the kitchen wall and place flat on the table. You can now fill the centre with fresh fruit and nuts — a stunning centrepiece.

Topiary

You don't have to be limited by size or height. Put a two-metre-tall topiary in a hall; increase the diameter of the support pole and width of the ball of flowers and foliage at the top; or come down in size to sit in the centre of a dining table: the same principles apply.

Materials: internal container (bucket, icecream container or tin); external container (basket, ceramic pot or terracotta pot); soaked dry foam block (Oasis) chicken wire; branch or piece of dowl; cocus fibre; garden foliage; dried flowers; spray paint; ribbon; 22 gauge floristry wire; plaster of Paris. (Work on kitchen floor or outside as excess water will drip).

1. Mix plaster of Paris (the directions are on the pack).

2. Secure branch in plaster in internal container and allow to set.

3. Wrap chicken wire like a parcel around soaked foam block, tie ends together with floristry wire.

4. Place foam block on top of branch or dowl, pushing foam down until top of wire rests on top of branch.

5. Cut foliage to approximately the same length and push into foam block. It is easier to start your ball by placing foliage at the four main points of your **square** foam block, then in the middle of each of the sides, then continue to fill until the wire and foam block is covered.

6. Place finished topiary into the external container and cover the top of the plaster and internal container with cocus fibre.

When your fresh topiary has dried out and is looking a little sad, add dried flowers — either picked and dried or bought from your local florist. Place flowers in the same way as you did the original foliage. You now have a permanent piece.

Another idea for Christmas is to spray paint the topiary and pole with silver, gold or whatever colour your theme may be and place wired bows of ribbon through the topiary after paint has dried. Make the ribbon tails longer on the bows placed near the base of the ball to adorn and soften the pole.

Janet Bourke and Nelson Pringle of Bloomey's, Sydney are happy to give advice on unusual ways of utilising flowers and foliage.

Coping with Kids
A NEED-TO-KNOW GUIDE

It takes a baby about eight weeks to recover from its own birth; it will probably take its parents the rest of their lives. It is extremely hard for a young woman, a single parent or a woman who has had several years in an interesting career to find herself back at square one, feeling totally inexperienced and ignorant, with a baby on her hands. In fact, we all know a lot more than we think we do about raising children and the biggest pitfalls are not ignorance but tiredness, frustrations about lack of time, loss of freedom and financial difficulties. So, how do you go about coping? Lynn Humphries has gathered some facts and ideas to help women with children not yet at school keep on top of motherhood.

Top 10 rules

1 Set aside time every day to play, read and talk to your children without any interruptions whatsoever. Being there isn't sufficient — it is the quality not the quantity of your care that counts.

2 Learn to say no. Some perverse streak in us all makes us believe we can handle an ever-expanding load. There has to be a cut-off point. Do not take on any work, either for your family or outside the home, that you cannot accommodate in your routine without it causing severe disruption.

3 Sleep when the baby sleeps. This point cannot be emphasised enough. Do not use these times to rush around putting things in the washing machine. Conserve your energy and be sure to rest when the baby does.

4 Learn from day one to re-order your priorities and expectations and to be prepared to compromise at all times.

5 Don't expect to have a tidy house. Clear up once a day only or you will drive yourself mad.

6 Lists, lists, lists. Make these all the time for pinpointing chores, shopping needs, necessities for outings.

7 Go out once a day with your children, no matter how much you've got to do in the home.

8 Don't make your children an excuse for not socialising. If you are asked to a friend's for dinner, put the baby in the bassinet and take it with you. At times you will feel that moving house is an easier occupation, but, allowing yourself to become housebound has no rewards. Enquire if there is a parent-run baby-sitting service in your area. If there isn't, start one up.

9 Take the time to give something back to yourself. Easier said than done, but you must maintain an interest outside the home or a hobby, even if you only get to attend to it once every two or three weeks. Join a Women in Touch group to meet others who wish to talk about anything *but* children. This organisation has branches in Victoria and Queensland and plans to extend groups throughout Australia. For details contact (02) 587 6686. If you are lonely, enquire about CWA, Red Cross or other organisations in your area. If there isn't anything, think seriously about organising some form of group meetings for women.

10 Take the time to give something back to your partner. Also easier said than done. Getting someone to mind the children for a couple of hours once a month so that you can meet for lunch will give you time to enjoy one another's company, discuss important issues without interruption.

Money

Children are wonderful; they are also expensive. The monthly Federal government allowance for a first child will just about cover the cost of milk and juice consumed by a one-year-old each month. In addition, the child will be eating something in the region of seven bananas, six apples, two chicken breasts, two large fillets of fish, vegetables, six eggs, bread, cereal, cheese and yoghurt every week. He will also need clothing, toys, furniture, toiletries and medicines. If you intend using some form of child care or pre-school facility, this will have to be costed into the family budget, too.

If you are a family with a very low income, have triplets, are a single parent or have a handicapped child, make sure you are receiving all the assistance to which you are entitled. For example, the Mothers/Guardians allowance is a special payment to sole parents; there are Health Care Cards offering various concessions to those on low incomes or who are receiving unemployment or special benefits. Contact your local Department of Social Security for information.

> **Prepare a safety kit the child can take everywhere. Include an identification card, list of important phone numbers, correct change for a phone call, even enough money for bus or taxi fare. Tape it to the inside of school bag or lunch box.**

Food

● Keep a good storecupboard to avoid frequent dashes to the takeaway or the corner shop. Only use these outlets as backups in an emergency.

● Always keep at least one precooked family meal in the freezer ready for those times when something prevents a fresh meal being cooked. For small children, freeze a couple of days' supply of something such as chicken stew and keep puréed, cooked vegetables, which have been frozen in ice-cube trays, packaged and labelled ready for use.

● If you have the space and the time, grow as many of your own vegetables as possible.

● Most children love biscuits, cakes, sweets and sugary drinks, but they are not a necessary part of their diets and are expensive. Don't encourage bad eating habits which can put children on the road to obesity and the dentist. Moderation is required.

● Always shop with a list or you'll end up with half the things you need and a lot of extras.

● If, like most parents, you shop and cook with children in tow, try to involve them in these activities. As horrifying as this may sound, it is sensible to get your children used to the idea, as early as possible, that you appreciate and need help.

● Shop outside the busy times such as late-night openings and Saturday mornings.

● Let your children choose which sort of breakfast cereal or yoghurt flavour to buy. This all takes time of course and patience.

● In the kitchen, encourage your children to weigh out ingredients for you and stir or roll things out where possible. Particularly when there is a new baby in the family, older children will love to know they are appreciated and are actually "helping" Mummy.

● If you haven't a clue what to cook for your babies and small children, get hold of one of the following: "Feeding your baby and young child in Australia: Birth to three years" by Virginia Phillips (Hyland House); "Feeding baby" by Jacki Passmore (Lansdowne); "Cooking for your baby the natural way" by Laraine Toms (Nelson). The Nursing Mothers Association issues helpful leaflets on nutrition.

Have an activities box with crayons, pencils, coloured paper (different textures as well), round-edged scissors, glue, scraps of fabric, ruler, string, magazine pictures so children will be able to find everything in the one place if they decide to draw or paint.

PAPER ART

The young artist has been inspired (perhaps) by the style and vibrancy of the great Matisse. Encourage children to be creative with paper — you'll need some in very cheerful colours and a firmer paper for the background, plus some glue. Method: Cut the motifs out of the bright paper with a firm hand. Arrange the vase, then the flowers on the background paper. Move them around until you arrive at what you like best — make it as colourful as an explosion of fireworks. All that's left to do then is to paste, very carefully, making sure that you don't put on too much glue. Keep scraps and offcuts of paper and fabric handy to keep children amused.

Cent Idees/Maltaverne/Faver/
World Press Network, 1986.

Clothes

- With a first child, the temptation is to buy far too many clothes; most of us learn the hard way. Buy very few items in tiny sizes — your child will quickly grow out of them.
- It's no disaster to put your children in hand-me-downs; personalise them with appliqués and embroidery if you wish. Most of the time, children need serviceable "working" clothes, so save your money for something for "best" and for those other expensive items such as shoes.
- Never hand down shoes as the shape of every child's foot differs and will mould a shoe to its own needs and shape.
- If you are good at sewing, enjoy and have the time to do it, go ahead and make some of your children's clothes. But, if it becomes another hideous chore which cuts into precious time when you could be doing something more rewarding, such as freelance paid work, then don't attempt it. There are no prizes for staying up half the night trying to get a dress finished for your daughter if you have the means to buy one ready-made.
- Go to end-of-season sales and buy ahead for the following year. Larger sizes can be put away.

Toys

It is a hard fact that, after paying a lot of money for a toy, your child will often be much happier playing with the box it came in. Grandparents are particularly prone to lavishing toys on a child; they would be better off giving good books which the child will cherish later in life, or helping out with the clothing requirements. Books such as "Play and your child" by Anne May (Nelson) and the Australian Women's Weekly "Children's Art & Crafts" are full of good, inexpensive ideas for making toys and playing games which will keep your child entertained and involved for many hours.

- Look into the possibility of borrowing toys, for a modest sum, from a toy library. A few have been set up in Australia — check your local phone directory or ask at your baby clinic if such a service exists in your area.
- If you are some distance from a good shopping centre, consider buying education toys through the mail. Johnson & Johnson produces a set of Child Development toys for young children which meet all Government standards for safety and durability. Once the age of your child is noted, two toys are sent to you every eight weeks which are specially designed to help the child develop particular skills. Write to Johnson & Johnson Pty Ltd, P.O. Box 252, Dee Why, NSW 2099 for details. Most good toy order shops issue catalogues of their stock and will sell through mail order.
- Count your blessings when your child starts taking an interest in books and, as soon as you can be sure he won't tear them up or chew them, enrol him in the local public library. It is never too early to instil a love of reading in a child.

Furniture

You could buy heaps of paraphernalia — there is a plethora of children's equipment on the market. Avoid gimmicky items and build up from the basics as you find it necessary. Where applicable, try to buy items approved by the Standards Association of Australia.

- Items such as highchairs and cots are expensive. Where possible, buy those models which convert into something else, for example, a cot which converts to a single bed with a chest of drawers; a highchair that converts to a desk and chair. Initially they may seem expensive, but they will pay for themselves in the long run.
- If you obtain furniture through your local newspaper or from friends, check that it is safe — see that latches are secure and that there are no splinters in a wooden playpen. Don't buy second-hand mattresses as every child moulds a bed to his or her own shape. Also, it can be very unhygienic.
- Shop around as prices vary greatly. If you see a well-priced item on special several months ahead of your needing it, snap it up and store it until required.

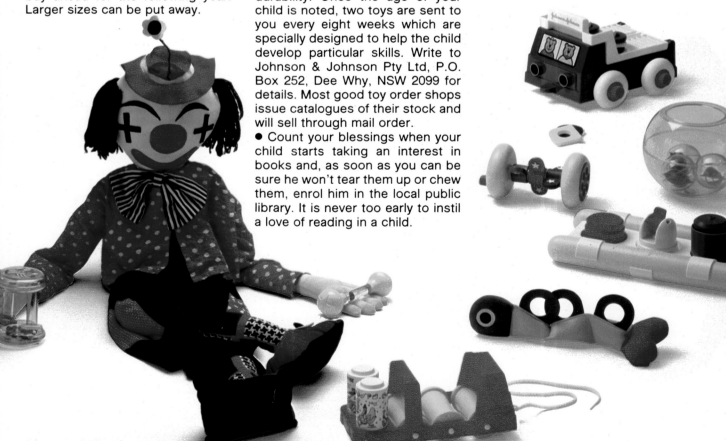

Toiletries

- Before buying bulk, ensure that your child is not allergic to a particular product. Your local clinic can advise on good products.

Health and safety

- Always have on hand the following local telephone numbers. Paste them inside your phone book and keep them beside the phone at all times. Make sure all the members of your family know where they are.
- Doctor (daytime and after-hours numbers)
- Baby health clinic
- Infant welfare sister (a midwife providing home post-natal care)
- Hospital
- Ambulance service
- Police station
- Poisons Information Centre: Sydney 519 0466; Brisbane 253 8233; Perth 382 8222; Canberra 43 2154; Melbourne 345 5678; Adelaide 267 4999; Hobart 38 8485; Darwin 20 8351
- The Nursing Mothers Association; National headquarters is at 5 Glendale Street, Nunawading, Victoria 3131, (03) 877 5011, counselling 878 3304. There are local groups in every state and territory (consult your phone book). The NMA helps with problems relating to breast-feeding, child care and nutrition. Booklets and leaflets are available. Group discussions take place in members' homes, to which non-members may go.
- Play school which your children are attending.
- Day care service which your child is attending.
- Any local backup organisations that could help with advice in an emergency, such as Karitane.
- Start taking your child to the dentist when he is about two and a half years old. At four he should have a ride in the dentist's chair; at five to five and a half, he should have his first clean and polish.

> **Assign a spot in the house — a shelf, cabinet or table — to a family member so that whatever is needed in the morning will be put there. Have a school box in the hallway or kitchen where all things for the following day's school are kept. This way they won't be forgotten in the morning rush.**

Childhood immunization

At 2 months: diphtheria, whooping cough, tetanus (triple antigen), poliomyelitis (sabin)

4 months: diphtheria, whooping cough, tetanus (triple antigen), poliomyelitis (sabin)

6 months: diphtheria, whooping cough, tetanus (triple antigen), poliomyelitis (sabin)

12 — 15 months: measles, mumps

18 months: diphtheria, tetanus (CDT)

School entry: diphtheria, tetanus (CDT) poliomyelitis. These boosters are given at entry to school, kindergarten or pre-school, provided it is at least 12 months since the previous doses have been given

15 years: diphtheria, tetanus (ADT), poliomyelitis

Enquire about First Aid courses from the Red Cross or St John's Ambulance Association in your State. Vital information such as resuscitation is very difficult to teach from a diagram — practical courses are an inexpensive investment in your family's welfare.

- Keep a supply of Medicare forms in your health file.
- Make your home as safe for your children as possible. Anticipate danger areas and do something about them before trouble arises.

Buy some, if not all, of the following: a tried-and-tested baby capsule for the car; a safety seat for the car (from five months — four and a half years); a silver chain with international medical symbol alerting doctors and hospitals to any allergies experienced by the wearer — allergies are engraved on the back; childproof safety catches for drawers and cupboards; wooden safety gates for the top and bottom of flights of stairs; protective plastic covering for three-point power sockets. The covers plug in and prevent children from poking objects such as screwdrivers into the holes; a protective sports helmet approved by the Standards Association of Australia for children riding bikes in the street.

- Obtain a poisons chart from your doctor or clinic. Paste it up inside the bathroom cabinet and ensure the whole family knows it is there in case of an emergency.

Medical records

If you have several children, or even if you only have one, it is difficult, if not impossible, to remember details about doctors' visits, innoculations, due dates for dental visits and all things relating to the family's health.

- Make a file for each member of the family, yourself included, put their name clearly on the front and store in it documents such as birth certificate, records of innoculations, details regarding general safety in the home (keep that in your file), and details of allergies.
- Keep a reminder list of the ages at which your children require various innoculations. Don't be lax in having these done. Some diseases such as measles and whooping cough are extremely dangerous in babies and your failure to innoculate your children could result in severe illness in another child who contracts the disease from your offspring. If parents don't bother to immunize their children because a particular disease has all but been eradicated, they risk being responsible in part for starting it up again.

To work or not to work

The reasons for mothers going back into the workforce when their children are young are twofold; financial necessity and the desire for mental stimulation and career advancement.

- A job, either one you can do from home or one outside it, is an additional source of stress to the day-to-day business of running a home and raising a family — it is a considerable energy drain. If you are hoping to go back to work before your children are of school age, consider the following.
- First, thrash out the issue with your family, pinpoint the possible areas of conflict and dissent and set about solving them before work gets underway and resentments and misunderstandings arise.

> **Label areas of wardrobes and drawers so that clothes can be found quickly and easily.**

Child care

Whatever kind of job you have, you are going, at some point to need to use some sort of child care facility. The facilities in this country are not extensive nor are they likely to become extensive in the immediate future. Your options are: creches which are either Commonwealth-funded or are commercially run (i.e. are profit-making); work-related care centres; family day care which is home-based care supervised by the local council; neighbourhood centres; pre-school and kindergartens; out-of-school hours and holiday care; private nanny services; relatives and friends.

● The cost, availability and number of hours of care given in each of these categories differs considerably. You will have to ascertain what the situation is in your own area, what money you have to pay for it and how much care you need before deciding what you would like to opt for. What must be stressed, particularly in respect of government and local council funded facilities is that the demand far exceeds the supply, and the earlier you put your child's name on the list, the better. Even if you don't think you will be needing care for a year, put your child's name down now. (The same applies if you are planning to give your child a private education. Registering your infant at birth is a sensible move.)

● If you are planning to return to your previous place of work, do not make unrealistic promises to your employer before you know exactly where you stand with day care. At time of going to press, one family day care centre in Sydney was placing babies (ie, children under 18 months old) in care at the rate of one every three months. If your child were tenth on the list, theoretically you would have 30 months to wait. Remember that if you have been working with an employer for a full year, you are entitled to 52 weeks' maternity leave without pay.

● Whatever system of care you use, check with a solicitor if you need to take out insurance against accidents to your child or damage caused by them in the place which cares for them.

> **Sweeten jobs around the house by providing a treat when a task has been completed well.**

Additional help

Chores don't go away, and if you're working outside the home, they'll still be waiting for you when you get back. Money is the great cure-all but few women are able to afford the backup services they would like to have.

● For those of limited means, seriously consider finding the spare cash for the following in an emergency, or when you really need a break: a nappy wash service (about $13 per week for a minimum of four weeks); a cleaner who will also help out with chores such as ironing; a window cleaner, or a gardener.

● And don't avoid asking your partner and older children to help. Don't let resentment at their inactivity build up into a blazing row. Deflect trouble by asking in a reasonable, rather than shrill manner, that you need and expect help.

> **If you are a working parent, have your children call you at work as soon as they get home. Make sure they keep you informed. If music lessons or football practice has been changed or they have to leave the house for a few minutes, they should let you know. Tell children not to use the phone at a pre-arranged time so that you can call them.**

What am I qualified to do?

If, after four years of looking after children, you believe the only thing you are any good at is cutting up food into tiny pieces, think again. Motherhood is as useful a qualification in many jobs as any examination pass. Mothers are constantly finetuning their organisational and management skills, they deal with conflict, handle the family budget and would be regarded as a star turn by any time and motion study. Doing several things at once, planning ahead and utilising one's energies intelligently equip a mother for many of the situations she will encounter in the work force.

The professional approach

Whether you are working full or part-time, make it clear when you are settling your terms of employment with your future employer that you are both in complete agreement about the hours you will be expected to work (and will be paid for) and establish how much, if any, out of hours commitment (attending functions, for example) you will be required to give. It is not fair to other employees to give the impression you will pull your weight, and then fail to do so.

Party giving

Before planning a birthday party, consider whether or not your child is old enough to enjoy it or even realise what all the fuss is about. For children under three or four, it is an event enjoyed more by the relatives than the child. Wait until your child is old enough to appreciate what is going on before you invite hordes of other little ones around.

● Always keep plans for your child's party very low-key. Weeks of anxious anticipation can often result in over-excitement, tears and disappointment.

● What sort of party shall we have? A "theme" can run through the event. For example, every child could be asked to wear something red, and all the decorations could be in shades of red. Fancy dress is a popular idea, but spare a thought for those parents who may not have the time, money or skills to make something for the occasion. Keep your ideas simple, for everyone's sake. For instance, each child could be asked to come in a funny hat rather than the full regalia of fancy dress.

● For older children, consider hiring a conjuror, a clown or a puppeteer as entertainment. Or, organise the children to conduct their own puppet show or little play. You could write a script and supply some costumes.

● If you don't feel up to having a swarm of children in your house, take a manageable group out for the afternoon. Go to watch the planes take off from your local airstrip; have a picnic with plenty of games at your nearest barbecue site; plan a short bush

- While you are at work, the fact that you have another life at home to sustain should have as little bearing on your performance as possible. Of course, there will always be emergencies and unforeseen occurences which necessitate your having time off. If you have always played fair with your employer, he will play fair with you.
- Do not feel guilty if you are working part-time while your colleagues are working full-time. You would not have been employed in the first place if your skills were not needed by the organisation.

A miscellany of tips

- If you don't already have a pet, wait until your child is at least three. Many animals need almost as much attention as a baby. And small children can be very rough on small animals.
- Enter your child on your passport soon after its birth. Don't wait until you are going overseas before you get around to it.
- Keep a file of information on places for family outings, annual events the children would like to attend. Cut relevant articles out of magazines and newspapers.
- Remember to change private health insurance to family cover.
- Reserve part of a lower shelf in the refrigerator to ease before-dinner-grumbles. Have carrot sticks, cheese, nuts, raisins, boiled eggs and lettuce there so children can make themselves nutritious snacks without interrupting you.
- If you have more than one child, send the younger ones to bed earlier — even if it's only 15 minutes — to show the older child a sense of fairness, that with age comes some privileges.

walk in a National Park; go to the cinema; plan a trip backstage at your local theatre; hire a bus (check you have the necessary driver's licence) and take the children to an historic building, fun park or beauty spot; go to an ice-skating rink, bowling alley.
- Little children like to play games. Make sure you have everything well planned with plenty of things of interest for the children to do and plenty of little prizes for them to win.
- Keep food simple — finger-food is best. Avoid complicated dishes that require a battery of forks and spoons. Use disposable everything — napkins, plates, cutlery and cups.
- Keep an eye on your own child to make sure he or she is not becoming obstreperous and over-excited. A short spell in the kitchen helping Mummy, away from the mainstream of events, should calm them down.
- If you have the space and the patience, set out paints and craft-making items and supervise the children in some creative project. Make sure mothers supply their offspring with overalls — a couple of mothers or fathers could come and help you maintain some order over chaos. Generally, though, it is better not to invite parents to a child's party; you will find yourself trying to conduct two parties rather than one, and paying insufficient attention to either.
- McDonald's has facilities for children's parties. Enquire at your local branch before descending on them with your party. Bookings will need to be made well in advance. Pizza Hut outlets are also used to catering for groups of children.

Become Money Wise
A BEGINNER'S GUIDE

Financial planning is vital for all women whether working in the home, or with careers outside. Even $10 gleaned weekly from housekeeping funds can give you a start to becoming an investor; $50 a week from your pay packet can put you on the way to buying a house. Financial consultant Virginia Dowd shows how to achieve financial goals and security you might never have imagined could be possible.

Are you keeping your head above water?

Payday comes all too infrequently for most of us. And when it does, the realisation that up to 50 percent of our pay packet has already been skimmed off by the tax man hits hard. Taxation isn't the only enemy of our savings: its best friend, and our worst, is inflation.

Kay was on a comfortable salary which pushed her up to the 43 percent taxation bracket. She thought she had her money hard at work for her, earning 14.5 percent in the credit union. What Kay didn't realise was that with inflation running at 8 percent, investments must return 15 percent per annum before there is a positive result. Anything below this rate of return leaves a negative result, meaning the value of savings is being decreased. In other words, your investments are not keeping up with inflation.

These days there are many investment alternatives available for the small investor. Superannuation, insurance bonds and unit trusts will all help reduce the hurt caused by the double whammy of taxation and inflation. A word of advice though, speak to an expert about your investment plans. Each investor has a different need because of individual lifestyle and circumstances.

The Women's Investment Network (WIN) is a group of licensed female financial advisers with offices in Brisbane, Sydney, Melbourne, Perth and Adelaide. For further details on WIN and the group's series of free monthly lectures in capital cities, contact (008) 77 7805 (toll free number).

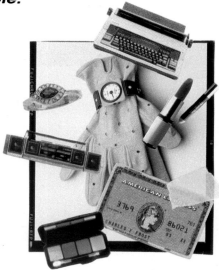

Taking your first steps successfully

Most fairytales end with a line that goes: And they lived happily ever after . . . but what about real life? If you've been brought up on this kind of dream, you may find it difficult to define your ideas in concrete terms — a vital first step to money success.

So where to start? Decide specifically what you want money to achieve for you:
- early retirement?
- a special holiday?
- a home of your own?
- financial independence?
- designer clothes?
- a tertiary education?
- overseas travel?
- flexibility to make a spontaneous decision.
- investments that produce income outside of the salary.

Spending time defining your goals now can save time and money later. Your personal aims will of course change with time, depending on your particular stage of life, but focusing on them and even putting some of them into words **now** is the first step in getting your self organized.

The next step is to make a financial plan which will enable you to achieve your goals. For this it is essential to get some expert advice. You will need to select investments which will make your money work for you and to decide how many dollars a week you will need to put aside to get your plan into action.

Choosing an investment and financial adviser is an important decision and one which can be one of the most rewarding you may ever make. Don't rush your decision. Shop around for someone you feel comfortable with because discussing your personal financial affairs and ambitions is a very sensitive matter. It's rather like shopping around for a good doctor who gives you honesty, trust and confidence. Ask advice from family and friends, acquaint yourself with the language of the money world by reading the investment pages of newspapers and magazines . . . Get a feel for what is going on. Then choose an adviser who can work closely with you planning for the future for the next five, 10, 15 years and in your retirement.

What is an investment portfolio?

A well-structured investment portfolio takes advantage of many investment and insurance options to suit an individual's needs. You should rely on a range of ways of putting money to work within the one portfolio — in other words, putting your financial eggs into several baskets. A portfolio should take advantage of different markets and take individual lifestyle requirements into account.

Making the decisions now!

Annabelle, a sales representative, is in her early 30s. With a salary of $27,000 Annabelle leads a glamorous lifestyle and travels frequently. Job requirements meant she spent most of her salary on clothing and entertainment.

Weighing up her life-long goals with a friend one day, Annabelle decided what she did want was a good deposit for a home by the time she was 40. Secondly, she and her boyfriend planned to have children when she was 37 which meant having enough money to educate them at tertiary level in 10-15 years time.

Finally, for her long term investments, Annabelle needed to commence contributions to a personal portable superannuation fund as soon as possible.

Annabelle and her investment adviser mapped out a savings plan which provided investment returns in five years for the unit, an education nest egg which would mature in 15 years and a plan for retiring with $200,000. All this was achieved on a saving of $50 per week only.

Of the $50 Annabelle was capable of saving each week, $20 was allocated for long term

superannuation benefits at today's rates of return. Annabelle's payout on retirement should be worth approximately $400,000.

A weekly $10 was invested in an insurance savings programme to give a tax free lump sum of around $15,000 in 15 years.

The remaining $20 per week was saved in an interest bearing account and once $1000 accumulated, was invested in various growth and income earning investments. After 7 years this should provide around $10,000, hopefully a useful deposit for a house or home unit.

Getting your house in order

When the house is a shambles, you're missing the basic cooking ingredients, the washing's piling up and the kids are sensing something is awry, it's tempting to give up and dive under the bedclothes and play dead. But sooner or later you'll have to face the day.

Budgeting is something like keeping your house in order. The longer you put off taking charge of it the more the overdue bills pile up and the nagging worry of rising costs gets to you. Keeping track of what money comes in and what goes out should become as natural a part of life as routinely taking the garbage out.

First draw up an account of where you are at the moment month by month. List what money comes in from salaries, dividends, interest on savings and investments. Then add up expenses: rent or mortgage, groceries, travel, and regular bills like telephone, power, insurance premiums, rates, school fees. Irregular costs such as clothing, entertainment, holidays, house and car repairs, furnishings, presents. Have a look at last year's cheque book stubs or credit card invoices as a check.

Now compare your income with your expenses. If you're just breaking even, it's time to take a long hard look at where your spending is out of control. Next, draw up a budget with the aim of generating more spare cash at the end of the month — part for emergencies and part for saving and investment.

It's important to get into that habit of budgeting a certain percentage to invest because this will help you prepare now to face the rest of your life. Breaking even just isn't good enough — it's like going fishing without a safety jacket.

Accurate budgeting helps us to determine exactly how much income we need to earn from our investments to provide us with a steady cash flow throughout the year, even over unexpectedly high expense periods.

BUDGET CHECKLIST

	ANNUAL COSTS	WHEN DUE	IMMEDIATE MONTHLY COSTS	LONG TERM MONTHLY COSTS	POSSIBLE INCREASES
HOME					
MORTG. PAYMENTS/RENT					
RATES					
GAS					
ELECTRICITY					
TELEPHONE					
MAINTENANCE					
INSURANCE					
TOTAL HOME					
CAR/TRANSPORT					
REPAYMENTS					
REGISTRATION					
INSURANCE					
MOTORISTS' ASSOCIATION					
TYRES					
PETROL/OIL					
REPAIRS					
FARES					
TOTAL CAR/TRANSPORT					
FOOD AND HOME GOODS					
MILK/BREAD					
MEAT/FISH					
FRUIT/VEGETABLES					
GROCERIES					
SCHOOL LUNCHES					
TOTAL FOOD					
OTHER NECESSITIES					
INSURANCE (LIFE/HEALTH)					
CLOTHES					
SCHOOL CLOTHES					
SCHOOL FEES/EXCURS.					
TOTAL OTHER NECESSITIES					
PLEASURE					
RESTAURANTS					
HOLIDAYS					
CINEMAS, SHOW, VIDEOS					
SPORT					
HOBBIES					
SUNDRIES					
TOTAL PLEASURE					

FOOD & HOUSEHOLD
(electricity, gas, phone)
30%

HOUSING
(mortgage, rent, rates)
25%

SAVINGS/LOANS
10%

INSURANCE
5%

EXTRAS
20%

CLOTHING
10%

WEEKLY BUDGET GUIDE
TOTAL 100%

	ANNUAL COSTS	WHEN DUE	IMMEDIATE MONTHLY COSTS	LONG TERM MONTHLY COSTS	POSSIBLE INCREASES
SPECIAL PURPOSE SAVINGS					
e.g. POOL, OVERSEAS HOLIDAY, NEW CARPET, ETC.					
TOTAL SPEC. PURPOSE SAVINGS					
TOTAL EXPENDITURE					
INCOME					
SALARY					
INTEREST					
BOARD					
FAMILY ALLOWANCE					
OTHER					
TOTAL INCOME					
CREDIT					
OVERDRAFT					
BANK LOAN					
CREDIT CARDS					
OTHER LOANS					
TOTAL CREDIT					

The prudent housewife

Kathy had devoted the past 20 years of her life to raising four children. During that period, Kathy managed the household finances, which were often tight, with the demands of four teenage children. A few years ago, Kathy realised that she too could have a small income of her own after hearing an investment adviser on a talk back radio show. Each week from then on, Kathy aimed to put aside $20 of family endowment or housekeeping money. Kathy adopted the principle of paying herself first — before the bills for school uniforms arrived or before she picked up the dry cleaning. Gradually this became a habit and by investing her $20 per week in an investment savings account, paying 10% per annum compounded monthly, Kathy built up her assets to reach $2,000. Her aim was to build up some capital and then expand her portfolio to achieve a good spread of investments.

Kathy moved her money into insurance bonds, with the help of her adviser, which provided good rates of return and tax advantages. Her intention was to bolster the family income as her husband drew closer to retirement. Not only did her funds grow but her interest in finance increased when she realised we don't all have to be financial whiz kids to play the money game successfully.

Put your mind into investor gear

How many times have you said to yourself: "there must be an easier way to make a living". Well, here's some good news, there is.

A person can only work eight to 10 hours a day, but a dollar can work for you non-stop, 365 days a year without you lifting a finger — if you invest it wisely.

Investing is not only a good idea for the woman who goes out of the house to earn an income. It is for all women. After all, we all have income of some sort. Adapting to the idea that anyone can earn income, but that it's what we do with that income that matters, is your first hurdle.

It's no longer good enough to "save for a rainy day" or to "look after your pennies and the pounds will take care of themselves". In today's volatile economic climate you can't afford to keep surplus cash under the mattress or in a low interest earning savings account. By the year's end you'll find inflation has eroded your financial position and that long awaited holiday or car is further away than you thought. Now is the time to put

your mind into investor gear and make your hard earned income accumulate and generate additional capital.

Investment can do these things for you:

● Maintain the purchasing power in future years of carefully accumulated funds.

● Give you a source of income other than wages in the form of regular interest income or accumulated capital gains.

● Achieve financial security and flexibility according to your income needs in your life.

A prudent investment program will insure against an uncertain future, achieve goals five, 10, 15 years ahead and allow for improvement of assets and lifestyles. So forget saving, think investment.

Investments grow and mature

with time like healthy plants. The longer the plant has to establish roots and flourish, the larger the plant will become. The compounding of interest on long term investments makes it imperative to start investing your savings now! Let the dollars you invest now start working for that future time when you no longer want to work.

Making your own silver spoons

When you haven't had a privileged background and have had to work hard for every cent, some imagine that the people with money are members of an exclusive club which you can't join unless you came into this world with a silver spoon in your mouth. But you don't need inherited wealth to enjoy some of life's riches. With a little planning you can become wealthy through your own efforts.

No matter what you earn, you too can become an investor. If you started in your early twenties, $20 a week in a superannuation fund could earn approximately $1,000,000 by the time you retire. But it's never too late to make decisions about superannuation.

BUILDING FROM THE BOTTOM LINE

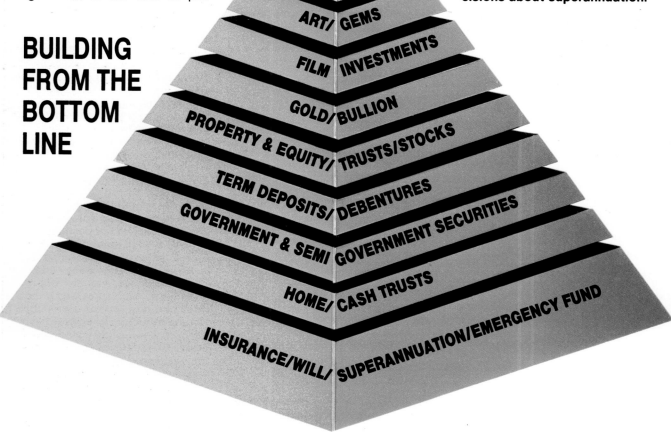

FUTURES

OTHER OPTIONS

ART/ GEMS

FILM INVESTMENTS

GOLD/BULLION

PROPERTY & EQUITY/ TRUSTS/STOCKS

TERM DEPOSITS/ DEBENTURES

GOVERNMENT & SEMI GOVERNMENT SECURITIES

HOME/ CASH TRUSTS

INSURANCE/WILL/ SUPERANNUATION/EMERGENCY FUND

The opportunities to invest are vast and every investment carries with it varying risks and rewards. Actually, setting up an investment portfolio is a little like planning a holiday. Firstly, you must decide what kind of holiday best fits your personality and requirements. What do you feel comfortable with? It's no good letting a travel agent give you the hard sell on a package tour of ancient ruins when you'd much rather be lying on a beach in the sun. Your investment decisions are just as individual and no matter what an investment adviser recommends, the final choice is yours.

Investments may be grouped into two broad categories — capital gain investments and interest bearing investments. Capital gain investments generally involve specific ownership (such as shares, growth unit trusts, real estate or collectibles such as stamps and coins, jewellery, art, gemstones and antiques). They are designed to generate a capital gain due to appreciation in value between the time you buy and sell, meanwhile offering some income such as share dividends and rent or no income as is the case with collectibles. These investments are attractive when you are trying to minimise personal income tax, but want something to look forward to in the coming years.

Loan investments seldom bring capital gain, instead they generate regular returns in the form of interest. They include bank, building society and credit union deposits, government bonds, company debentures, unsecured notes. Interest rates are fixed (for the term of the investment) or variable (subject to fluctuations in market rates).

The list of what you can invest in doesn't end there. You can invest in anything from fat lamb futures to Ming vases, micro chips to macadamia nut plantations. And remember to review your investment portfolio regularly — at least annually.

How not to drown in debt

While you may think that the quickest (and most satisfying) solution to your credit problem is taking a pair of scissors and cutting up your credit cards, it doesn't achieve much in the long term.

Credit is a fact of life in the 80s and if used wisely can iron out the bumps between pay cheques. The fact still remains that whatever we borrow must be paid back — with interest. And sometimes those charges can be crippling. Things start to go wrong when we start regarding what we've borrowed as our own. It's such an easy pattern to fall into.

We mustn't forget that financial institutions make their money out of the interest you pay on the money you borrow — they are not after all being charitable when they suggest you might like to increase your credit card limit. Don't be drawn into a vicious circle; stay on the sidelines and in control of your credit cards.

Credit card do's and don't's:

● **Do** make full use of credit cards as a short term means of extending your buying power, if it is cheaper than obtaining a normal personal loan, or you don't have the collateral for a personal loan.

● If you already have a large amount owing, **don't** make any more purchases on credit until you find out what your minimum monthly repayments will be.

● **Do** meet your minimum monthly repayment, as failure to do so not only incurs more interest, it will eventually damage your credit rating and mean you miss out on buying your dream home, car, or trip overseas.

● **Don't** be blind to the fact that interest is charged on your debt — even if it seems insignificant, all those dollars and cents add up.

● **Do** think hard before you use your credit card. Ask do I really need this now? Do I really need this at all? What you save today could buy you something really important tomorrow.

● **Do** look on credit as a source of cash for emergencies, but make sure that you will be able to repay the debt as quickly as possible once the situation changes.

Judy is a 30-year-old up and coming executive. Streetwise when it comes to finances, she makes planning and achieving financial goals seem easy.

She has developed an interest in the financial pages of the paper. She participates in the investment market and understands its cycles.

Although Judy lives comfortably on a $30,000 salary, she resists luxuries. Despite this, she is always dressed well because her three-year-old mix and match wardrobe is timeless.

Judy is fully committed to the investing mentality. She has planned her investments with her own personal real estate and $5,000 invested in cash management trusts and mortgage trusts.

Also interested in property and equity trusts, Judy does her homework and investigates their suitability to her needs. With her financial adviser, she looked at the prospectus of many trusts and selected public equity and property trusts because of the security offered — these trusts are scrutinised by State Corporate Affairs Commissions. By investing in these trusts she achieved a spread of investments which meant flexibility, liquidity and potential for financial growth.

To buy or not to buy

For most single women in the workforce, saving for a home is given a low priority after clothes, car and travel. This is probably because we usually pigeon-hole buying a home with marriage and raising a family — something we'll think about if and when it happens.

But as rents continue to escalate with inflation is it wise to put off buying your own home? In the past, women were discriminated against by banks and other lending institutions; they could not apply for a home loan unless they had a male guarantor. These days however this is no longer as difficult; banks and building societies are welcoming applications from women who are solely responsible for their own financial well being.

It is also true that interest rates on home loans have escalated in recent years along with rents; however you only need to compare the effects of renting and buying to realise which way makes the most of your money.

RENTING

If your current rent is now $100 a week, with inflation you can expect that weekly rental to rise by an average of 5% per year over the next 25 years. In that time you would have paid out *$240,000* in rent . . . a week's rent buys a week's shelter. Nothing more. At the end of 25 years you will own . . . *nothing.*

ESTIMATED COST OF RENTAL IN 25 YEARS' TIME:

If rentals increase by the expected 5% per year, at the end of 25 years you would be paying rent at the rate of . . . *$340 a week.*

BUYING A HOME

Even if you borrow $50,000 over 25 years, your repayments, including interest at 14.5% would be less than *$190,000*

If the home you buy costs $55,000 now, and even if it increases only a 5% per year (compounded), in 25 years it could be worth *$180,000.* (Even if your home stayed at its present value — which it won't — you would have acquired a very worthwhile asset.)

ESTIMATED OUTLAY IN 25 YEARS' TIME:

Apart from rates, maintenance and house insurance, costs will be nil.

Saving for a home

Now aged 21, Virginia left school three years ago and spent some of that time unemployed. She experienced disheartening job knockbacks. She felt keenly the problems of living in this society with severe financial restrictions. Her determination to secure a good job eventually won through and she's very aware of the security her job offers her.

Because she was unemployed, Virginia knows what it is like not to have choices and money. As soon as she commenced her job, she began to adopt an investor mentality — she saved hard.

On a wage of $16,000 and still living at home, Virginia put away $11,000 in three years. Slowly her savings are mounting up in a bank account. Putting away a portion of her salary in a moderate interest bearing bank account has suited Virginia in the short term. It gives her an immediate feeling of security and increases her chances of getting a housing or car loan. In other words, she is building a savings track record with the bank.

In the long term, however, any investment that features a high degree of accessibility offered by banks, usually provides low real interest returns.

The combined effects of inflation and taxation make it unwise for Virginia to leave the majority of her funds in a savings account over a long period. However, Virginia wisely chose to maintain her potential borrowing capacity by leaving some of her capital in the bank. At times when banks are awash with money for loans, building up a track record isn't the necessity it has been in the past for first home owners. If, however, Virginia decided to settle down in two years' time the situation may have reversed and Virginia may find herself with no recourse if the bank rejected her loan application through lack of a savings record.

Virginia's mother helped her find the best options for the remainder of her assets in order to protect the purchasing power of her savings. At the same time however, Virginia's funds had accumulated and in order to reduce her future tax bill, she was advised to invest some of her funds in capital growth rather than income areas.

Virginia set out her goals and one of the high priorities was to put aside enough money so that when she is married she will have a sum to contribute to the purchase of a family home.

The options available to Virginia are numerous. She chose to invest wisely in a cash management and a first mortgage trust. The advantages of these options are twofold. Firstly, both options offer higher interest rates and consequently higher real returns than bank or building society savings accounts. And secondly both funds are accessible in case of emergency. Cash management trusts are accessible within 24 hours of your demand, whereas first mortgages usually have a waiting period of seven-14 days.

As well, Virginia may choose to put a portion of her funds into an equity trust for three to five years, which would also help to reduce her provisional tax bill.

Real estate investment

Having successfully crossed the barrier from tenant to landlord and laid your money on the line for your own home you may still have funds to invest.

Most of us are eager to make a good, solid, above average return. But unless you have a good knowledge and a fair degree of skill in this market, other investment options can generally provide safer and less volatile returns.

The basic problem with home owners investing the majority of their assets in domestic real estate today is that it breaks the most important rule in prudent investing, "don't put all your eggs in one basket." By diversifying your investments into other areas you are reducing the risk and potential disaster that a major decline in any one market will have on your portfolio.

But don't be completely discouraged by real estate investment. Many of the well balanced portfolio's still include real estate, but it is commercial real estate rather than domestic that you should go for.

Good quality commercial real estate has proven over many years to be the most secure and least volatile investment in protecting the purchasing power of money in Australia. This class of real estate is made accessible to the small investor by means of unit trusts. Property trusts can be tailor made for you to suit your personal investment objectives. The other beauty of trusts is that they are professionally managed funds.

His and her bank accounts

Married bliss doesn't always last forever. While it is difficult to protect yourself against unforeseen circumstances, in addition to the undoubted emotional strain of the time, you may have unwittingly left yourself financially vulnerable when things fall apart.

The joint bank account is one way of making your financial arrangements less shaky should unexpected circumstances arise. The essence of the joint account is equality. Both parties can contribute equally into the account for items purchased jointly. Aside from this, both parties are still able to operate personal accounts in tandem with the joint account.

Joint accounts also protect the separate interests of both participants. They do this by stipulating that although either party can deposit funds into an account, **both** parties must sign cheques for withdrawals. In this way, both people are aware of the account transactions. This is known as a both-to-sign account.

There is a second type of joint account, which either can operate, giving more freedom of access. In this account, any party can deposit funds and any party can withdraw funds from the account — but we wouldn't recommend this way of managing money.

The joint bank account allows for sharing as well as the vital protection of interests.

When there's a will, there's a way

Drawing up a will is essential, whatever your age or financial situation. While many people plan for certain events, only one-third of Australians anticipate the one event which is guaranteed to happen.

Once you've begun to build up your assets and protect them from excess taxation, the next step is to protect them for your heirs. Considering the time and energy used to build up a sound investment portfolio and your emotional investment in your family, it makes good sense to have a will.

A will is a vital tool that ensures your investments are protected after your death. It lets you choose your beneficiaries and designate how you want your estate divided.

For legal costs of $50 — $200, depending on time spent and complexity of the will, potential difficulties can be dispersed with.

Wills should be reviewed annually as your circumstances will change significantly over the years. Both spouses should have a will. Some people work under the mistaken belief that joint ownership of property will provide their partner with all their assets in the event of death. It doesn't work that way.

If you die without a will, which is called dying intestate, your assets are distributed according to the laws of succession. This process can be costly; it takes a lot of time and, in some cases, an investor's estate has even been forfeited to the Crown.

To write a will:
1. See a solicitor. Don't try to do it yourself as it may prove invalid for some reason.
2. Decide who will be the executor of the will.
3. List all the assets you own and how and to whom you want them distributed.

If you are making a will that doesn't include your intention to marry, a new will must be drawn up by a qualified person as the first one will be revoked. If you are separated but not divorced, you must make a new will if you do not want your estate to go to your former partner.

A super future

A vital component in any sound financial plan, believe it or not, is to consider your retirement. Whatever your age it is not too soon to plan for this time of your life. After all, when the income suddenly stops, the bills keep on coming. By putting away just $20 per week of your now income, you could avoid having to rely on government hand-outs and living below the poverty line in your old age.

With the government seriously questioning how they can afford even the social security bill, women of the 80s are now waking up to the benefits of long term financial planning as a way of avoiding the poverty trap. They are achieving this by joining superannuation schemes and wisely paying now to support themselves in the future.

If you are already a member of a company superannuation fund, make sure you fully understand your rights. Ask questions such as: What sort of interest is my money earning?; What if I was retrenched or resigned?; What is the fund's performance like each year?

Some companies use superannuation to keep their staff and if you leave before a certain period you may not get the full interest rate or the company contribution.

If you change jobs with a non-portable scheme, resist the temptation to spend your super payout. The payment can be rolled over into another super scheme, an approved deposit fund or a deferred annuity within 90 days without loss of any benefits.

If however, you are yet to join a fund, you should seriously consider a personal portable fund.

The biggest benefit of personal portable superannuation schemes to women is their flexibility. The employee can move between jobs or take time out to have a family without losing what they've already saved and you get the full performance value of your investment.

Superannuation contributions can alleviate some of your tax burden and provide a secure nest egg for your retirement.

Before joining a fund, firstly seek advice from a credible investment adviser as to which is the best fund to join. And secondly, ensure your contribution keeps up with inflation. Increase your contribution by 8% or 10% each year and that way a half a million dollars payout today will have an equivalent worth when it comes time for your payment. Due to the tax advantaged nature of end benefits and the tax exempt status of earnings in the fund, individuals should maximise contributions to a super scheme during their working life rather than relying on selling the family home to maintain lifestyle during retirement.

Protect your greatest asset

Most of us protect our cars and our homes from damage. Statistics prove however that few women protect their most valuable asset: their ability to earn an income.

Disability insurance that pays you when you can't work as a result of unforeseen injury or illness is one of the most valuable and necessary safeguards around.

Sara, a deserted 38-year-old mother of two, was involved in a car accident and serously injured. Off work and recuperating for 10 weeks, Sara's disability insurance paid for 75 percent of her normal average income and she was able to recover in peace knowing the major bills were taken care of. She couldn't eat out anyway or shop for clothes so the other 25 percent of her income wasn't really missed.

There are numerous policies available today to protect your salary in case of catastrophe but the important thing is to shop around and not take the first package that comes along. There are three basic questions to ask before making your decision and premiums will vary according to the answers.
1. How much insurance do you need? This will depend on how much you need to live on — work it out on the necessities plus a little in reserve. Not your full salary.
2. How long do you have to wait for benefits to be paid after the accident or illness? This can vary from seven days to two months. It depends on how long you can afford to be without an income and what your company will cover for you.
3. How long do you want to be paid for? — it can be one, two, five years or even life in case of a permanently debilitating accident or illness.

Protecting your family

Whether to take life insurance is one of the most difficult decisions we will ever have to make. Death is not something our culture can cope with anticipating. But the reality is that a premature death can devastate a family's financial situation.

Life insurance is a protection for those around you who might have to ruin their own savings plans if you die leaving debts and mortgages. Life insurance can replace lost income, provide funds for housekeeping, child care, or living expenses of aged parents or dependants.

When considering the type of policy you want, first decide:
1. How much money you want to leave your dependants?
2. Will they require more or less as time goes on?
3. How will you pay?
4. Will your income change?

Traditionally, life insurance policies were made up of a mixture of protection and investment. Those called "life insurance policies" covered the insured even past age 85. Where these whole-of-life policies were of a limited premium nature (ie paid to a certain age), premiums ceased, and upon death of the insured the sum assured was paid out. The policy holder could borrow against these policies.

However, due to a number of problems occurring in real life — as opposed to insurance salesmen projections — such policies have largely been replaced by (a) unbundled contracts which separate the death cover from the investment element, (b) straight term insurance contracts where the death benefit is payable should death occur during the term of the contract.

There is no saving element in term contracts so the policy cannot be borrowed against nor will there be any death cover after the expiry of the term. In most cases, you should select an amount which if invested at a reasonable earning rate will replace your income. Annual premiums increase with age. Premiums are much less for non-smokers.

SPENDING OVERSEAS

Poor planning and genuine emergencies are the main sources of problems for short-term overseas travellers. The three main ways of making sure that you have spending money while you're away are travellers' cheques (unless you are intending to spend large amounts, they should form the bulk of your funds), foreign currency notes and credit cards. Travellers' cheques are readily negotiable, usually refundable and available in most currencies. Check with your bank for the most acceptable currency with the most advantageous exchange rate. Major credit cards are accepted at airlines, hotels, restaurants, shops and banks around the world — they are an essential part of any traveller's survival kit. However, not all of these accept all cards. Find out which are most acceptable in the countries you plan to visit.

Shopping strategies

A few tips to take any pain out of what should be a pleasure:
● If you live in a major city, visit several duty-free stores to compare prices — they vary considerably.
● If you're buying cosmetics to take with you, check prices in the city duty-free stores and at the airport over the phone. Sometimes there are bargains you wouldn't want to miss.
● Before you go, make a list of what you really want to buy. Check the prices, both regular and duty-free. If the price is good and you don't mind toting it with you, buy it here; you're guaranteed of being able to take it back if anything goes wrong. If you don't buy it here, remember to carry a copy of the prices with you.
● Try not to buy just because it's there and it's inexpensive. Do you *really* want/need it? Equally, don't miss something you'll never see again. Learn to pounce.
● Don't buy first up. Case the joint. Compare prices. Take as much time as possible.
● Don't buy the right thing in the wrong place. You wouldn't go shopping for electronics in Bali, or diamonds in Tahiti, or Gucci in Paris, would you? Check what's good where.
● Take a calculator with you, or make yourself a ready reckoner you can refer to. It's very easy to get excited in one of those meganought currencies and think you're getting a bargain, when in fact it definitely isn't.
● Don't spend endless time looking for just the right shoemaker or tailor in a place like Bangkok or Hong Kong. They're all very good, as long as you know what you want. Insist on a fitting.
● Make sure you can carry it, or you'll be spending all the money saved on porters (and often, there isn't one). If it has to be shipped home, is it worth the extra money, or would you be better off buying it at home? Come to think of it, *would* you buy it at home?
● Try not to buy multiples of anything unless they're for gifts.
● Take a small spiral-bound (spine, not top) notebook. Before you leave, clip it into an indexed diary for each place you visit, using each right hand page as a diary (appointments, transfer times, air flight numbers), the page opposite for the notes you collect during that day (addresses, prices, things to remember). At the back of the book keep a running tally on how much you spend each day. Beats keeping all those separate pieces of paper.
● Try to develop "The Eye". A good international shopper can go back, unerringly, three days later, to a shop on the third level of a confusing arcade, and find that designer cream silk shirt.

Tapping your Resources
MONEY SAVERS

Whatever happened to good old-fashioned thrift? In the mass-produced, throwaway 80s, the word sounds as dated as warming pans and washboards. But thrift has lots going for it. It's the way to make extra money for worthwhile projects (an adventure holiday? riding lessons for the kids? an extra bedroom?). And it can be enjoyable. Paula Goodyer presents some tried-and-true money-savers.

How to save on children's clothes

RECYCLING YOUR OWN WARDROBE

● Before you toss out your outdated clothes, stop! They may fit your daughter. The tops we wore in the 70s were skinnier than they are today, so the T-shirt that's unfashionably tight on you could make a loose top for an eight to 10-year-old, or a denim shirt make a nifty jacket to wear with jeans.

● Adult T-shirts make fun nightdresses for small children too. Some items can be cut down to size — chop off the flares from an old pair of jeans and you've got the makings of a girl's denim skirt; fabric from a generously cut skirt or dress or man's shirt can make children's or even doll's clothes.

BUYING SECONDHAND

● There's a kind of thrill in sorting through a pile of secondhand children's clothing at a jumble sale/fete/thrift shop and finding a barely worn, hand-knitted sweater or a crisp nightie for 50 cents. Gems like these are there if you're prepared to look. And do forget any outdated notions about used clothes being tacky: secondhand can mean good fashion as well as money sense. And think what you can do with what you save.

● Bargains abound among used children's clothes because they outgrow things so fast they're thrown out before they reach the shabby stage. Although the least-worn clothes make the best buys, denim can be an exception — nicely faded jeans, skirts and pinafores make good play clothes that cost little. Always think ahead when you're buying — remember that the bargain that dwarfs your two-year-old now will fit in a few years.

OTHER GOOD SECONDHAND BUYS

● If you're browsing for clothes, don't forget to look for pre-loved toys and books. Although secondhand soft toys don't wear well, hardier things like prams, cars, construction toys and dolls' houses do. A naked doll might look forlorn, but imagine the transformation if you dress her up.

● New books are expensive, but go secondhand and you can build up an impressive children's library for a few dollars.

● Before you part with $200 for a child's bike, check what's for sale in the classifieds. Bikes are often quickly outgrown and used ones are available in good condition.

Entertaining children on the cheap

Children's playthings needn't cost the earth. In fact the more you improvise, the more you'll help your child to be resourceful and imaginative. Some ideas:

● A 'USEFUL' BOX.

● My useful box is actually a cupboard and when you open it, a small avalanche of old Christmas wrappings, cards, matchboxes, wood shavings and cotton reels tumbles around your ankles. It's a catch-all for anything a child can use for making things and can be built up gradually over the years. The contents are a useful back-up for rainy days and school holidays or even for babies too small to make things — you can use items (safe ones, of course) to fill a "surprise" bag or box for them to rummage through.

SUGGESTIONS FOR FILLING YOUR OWN USEFUL BOX:

● Small cardboard boxes (for making trucks, dolls' cribs)

● Scraps of fabric, wool, lace and patterned wrapping paper (for collages); buttons, braid

● Old magazines and cards for cutting out; old photos

● Corks (slice into discs to make wheels for a matchbox truck)

● Pasta (for collages, threading on to string)

● Shells, stones, pegs

● Crepe paper, tinsel

● Flour (to mix with water and little food colouring to make "cakes"). There's no limit to what children can make — for ideas see the Australian Women's Weekly Children's Art and Crafts Book or check the craft books in your library. Here are some ideas to start you off:

● Cut out "doll" shapes from cardboard and supply fabric scraps, wool, braid or cotton wool — your child can glue them on for clothes and hair.

● Save milk and cream cartons of all sizes. Cover in plain paper and let your child draw doors and windows on them to create a milk carton "city". You can add to this with roads (drawn on paper or card), cars, traffic lights (colour red amber and green spots on a paddle-pop stick and anchor in plasticine).

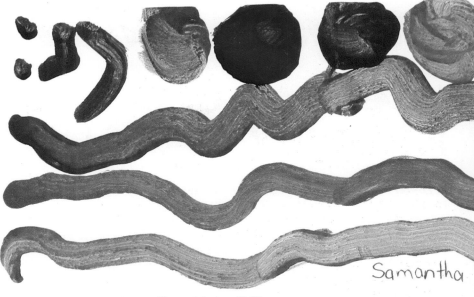

Samantha

PAINTING

● It's cheap, satisfying and keeps children amused for long periods. Although the initial outlay for children's paints (powder or liquid) costs money, they're an investment that lasts for months. You only need three colours to start (red, yellow and blue — mix the last two to make green). As well as painting on paper (or stones, egg cartons, or cardboard cylinders from kitchen paper) children can have a lot of fun creating different colours when they mix the paints.

● Using white flour will both extend powder paint and make colours paler; if you can afford them,

black and white paints will enable children to lighten and darken colours. You can also make your own paint by mixing flour and food colouring with water.

● To keep up with the demand for paper, never discard anything with a blank surface — the backs of old calendars, cards, junk mail, butcher's paper. Be nice to anyone with access to a photocopier — they can bring you the rejects from the waste bin. Some newspaper offices sell off the ends of newsprint reels — these give you metres of blank paper very cheaply.

DRESS-UP BOX

Every child needs one. Fill with the best variety of clothes, hats, accessories and props you can find. Besides your own and family cast offs, jumble sales are a good source. Vary the clothes as often as you can and don't forget accessories such as spectacles (minus the glass), ties, handbags, belts, flowers and feathers. You can make crowns, swords, pretty fairy wings by cutting out a cardboard shape and covering with foil, or improvise a space helmet by cutting a wine cask box down to size and covering that with foil.

CLAY

● Digging their fingers into clay and kneading it has a lot of appeal for children from toddlers upwards (why else have kids made mud pies for centuries?).

● You can buy potters' clay very cheaply from a pottery or craft supply shop. You can also find clay if you take a bush walk after it has rained (look for grey or ochre-coloured mud).

● Small children can roll clay into balls or pat it into pancakes which they can decorate by making patterns with a stick or studding with leaves and gumnuts. Balls can be made into beads — skewer with a sate stick to make a hole while they're still wet. Let them dry in the sun or a slow oven before painting.

● Older children can make pots by rolling the clay into "snakes" between their hands. The snakes are coiled into circles and piled on top of each other to make a coil pot. To stick the coils together or any other bits of wet clay use a little clay thinned with water to the consistency of double cream. They can also mould clay around shapes such as mugs and jars, or "pinch" it into simple bowls.

● Unlike clay fired in a kiln, sun or over-dried clay is fragile, so handle with care.

MAKE-UP BOX

Stocked with discarded lipstick, blusher, eye pencil and shadows, this will keep girls (and often boys) occupied for hours. Always supervise small children who may decide to "make-up" your walls, and help with any eye make-up — even older kids can get shadow in their eyes. Don't give mascara or eyeliner.

Other ideas

● Create extra storage or plant holders by spraying old baskets in white or pastel gloss — this camouflages even the shabbiest baskets.
● Unbleached calico must be the cheapest fabric available yet it makes effective furnishing fabric (for cushions, curtains, upholstery) especially teamed with natural textures like timber or stone.
● For stylish window-dressing without the cost of curtains, buy a length of cheap fabric (lining material, cheesecloth, calico, perhaps), wind it around a cornice pool leaving a drop of fabric at each side of the window. For extra dash make the drops longer than the distance between cornice and floor — this lets the fabric gather in soft folds on the floor.

Save on gifts

It's the thought, not the outlay, that counts. Instead of buying an expensive present, you could:
● Pot herbs in terracotta pots (start them well in advance so they're flourishing when you give them away).
● Buy plain white singlets for a new baby and decorate with your own embroidery, trim with lace or ribbon inserted around neck.

● Make batches of playdough in assorted colours for a toddler's birthday.
● Make inexpensive notebooks, diaries, address books special by covering them in pretty fabric.
● Give a button box — facelift a plain-lidded basket by trimming with lace and decorating the lid with buttons.
● Decant homemade vinaigrette or herb vinegar into a pretty bottle.
● Make a set of book plates using "parchment" notepaper decorated with pressed flowers.
● Give time: an afternoon's baby-sitting for a frazzled friend.

Co-operate and save

There are ways in which families can work together to save money:
FOOD CO-OPERATIVES
The idea is for a number of families to get together and buy food cheaply by buying in bulk from a wholesale greengrocer, produce market or butcher. It works on a roster system so that one person (or family) is responsible for buying the co-op's vegetables or meat for a week and dividing it up. To start your own co-op you need reliable members and a suitable wholesaler (check the Yellow Pages).
BABYSITTING CO-OPERATIVES
● A free babysitter saves heaps on the cost of a night out. To start a baby-sitting co-op you need eight or 10 couples or single parents which you should try and build to a team of 12 to 20. You can work on a points system of say four points to an hour — if you go out for three hours, you're in debt to the co-op for 12 points and the sitter is owed 12 points next time she wants to go out. Set a limit on how many points a member can use or save. If members go too far into the red, they have to baby-sit before they can use the co-op again. Have a roster system so each member has a turn at being the organiser for one month — members contact the organiser when they need a sitter. The organiser then rings the other members to see who's available — starting with those who are most in debt with the co-op.
Make sure co-op members don't all belong to the same social club or have children all going to

the same school — come the P & C Christmas party or the squash club dance you'll have problems.
SHARE-A-GADGET
Halve the cost of buying an appliance you don't need every day by sharing one with a responsible friend or neighbour. This works quite well with lawnmowers, carpet shampooers, even sewing machines, provided you agree to share on repairs.
STITCH THE FAMILY CAST-OFFS INTO A QUILT
Blankets are expensive, but the fabric from old clothes costs nothing. Besides warming the bed, you'll have a colourful "family history" of the clothes you all loved wearing.
SAVE THE PRICE OF HOUSEHOLD CLEANERS:
● Make your own furniture or floor polish. Grate 30g of beeswax in a jar and pour 140ml of turpentine over it. Stand in a warm place or in a saucepan of water over low heat until wax dissolves.
● Clean brasses quickly and cheaply by soaking them in about one tablespoon cream of tartar dissolved in two litres of warm water.
● Deodorise a stale room not with commercial sprays that get up your nose, but a drop of eucalyptus or lavender oil wiped over surfaces.

Other money savers

● Recycle a wine cask. Use the cardboard cover to make magazine holders. Cut away the bottom of the cask plus two-thirds of one of the long narrow sides. Decorate with patterned adhesive or wrapping paper.
● Grow your own beansprouts. For the price of one pack of ready-grown alfalfa or mung beans from the greengrocer, you can buy enough dried beans from the health food shop to sprout the equivalent of three packs. First soak dried beans for 24 hours in an old margarine tub. Then cover the tub with the sort of net greengrocers use for packaging fruit. Double it and secure with a rubber band. Place container upside down to drain beside your sink — so you'll remember to rinse beans once or twice daily. Harvest in three to four days.

MONEY-SPINNERS

Do you have a skill to sell? There are enterprising women in every suburb and country area making money from a home-based service or skill. Firstly, decide what you can provide that people in your area need.

TURN CREATIVITY INTO CASH

Living in an age of mass production has generated a demand for individual handcrafts — home-sewn cushions, quilts, baby clothes, decorative nappy holders, hand-painted ribbons and T-shirts, hand-made picture frames, lampshades and dolls' clothes. Some women sell their work privately by word of mouth, others sell to gift or decorator shops. Some have become so successful they have branched out into shops of their own.

One of the greatest money-spinning cottage industries of all just now is the making of health-style cakes and biscuits for supply to cafes, delicatessens and coffee shops. Banana, zucchini, carrot cakes, oatmeal-style biscuits or biscuits and cakes featuring muesli are sure sellers. Quiches, dessert tortes and individual pork pies are also in demand.

To handpaint a garment, use water-based fabric paint, available from art or craft shops. When you've painted your design, leave it to dry for 10 minutes, either in the sun or in front of a heater. When dry, make it colourfast by ironing it. Then simply wash it according to the directions on the fabric. T-shirt and matching shirt by artist Robyn Chadwick are available from Lavender Blue, Cremorne, NSW.

Ask them how they began and the stories are the same: a friend admired something they'd made, ordered one and their reputations spread. (It was Laura Ashley's home-sewn decorator cushions that launched her success.)

You don't have to be a genius either — being a competent sewer with good taste will do. Or you can always improve a so-so talent by taking a course. One woman who spent two terms at art school years before, refreshed her skill with a course of Chinese brush painting. She now earns extra money hand-painting greeting cards, wedding invitations and T-shirts.

Another friend filled her spare time making baskets and Christmas decorations from flour and water dough which she baked in the oven and glazed — and found the orders came rolling in.

Where do you start? Show off your handiwork to friends and gauge their response; hold a "party" and see what you can sell — a good idea before Christmas when people are in the market for gifts. See if you can interest any specialty shops in your work. If you can produce something unusual so much the better. For sources of inspiration, check decorator shops, local and overseas women's magazines as well as craft and decorator magazines.

WHAT SERVICES CAN YOU PROVIDE?

As the number of working mothers grows, so does the demand for services like ironing, baby-sitting and cleaning. Working couples have less time for jobs like painting, wallpapering, curtain making, altering clothes, gardening, home maintenance and mowing the lawn. Some couples may not need a regular cleaner, but need help for one-off jobs like oven and window cleaning or grand scale spring cleaning, so it pays to offer a range of services. Many women need someone who can reliably fill the multiple role of baby-sitter, cleaner and ironer (a wife, in other words).

Advertise what you can offer in the local press and/or community notice boards.

BE A HOUSE MINDER OR PET SITTER

Offer to water plants, feed pets, collect mail, mow lawns for holidaying householders.

OFFER A CHILDREN'S PARTY SERVICE

What a working parent wouldn't give for someone willing to bake a cake, make a batch of chocolate crackles and organise the games for a children's birthday party.

WHAT CAN PEOPLE LEARN FROM YOU?

Adults and children like learning something new and there's a demand for tuition especially in areas where organised courses are less available. You could teach: music, art, a language (including English for migrants), photography, cooking (health food or an ethnic specialty, even bread baking), sewing, embroidery, horse riding, dancing (tap, folk, jazz ballet), yoga, aerobics, self-defence, or coach a sport or school subject.

*Draw or paint greeting cards, as **at right**, and sell through specialty shops.*

*Make a dough basket, **above**, or any other decorative item from flour and water dough.*

48

BECOME A SECONDHAND CLOTHES DEALER

Beg or buy good quality used clothes and accessories from friends and thrift shops and resell at a profit. Hold seasonal collections in your own home.

BE A DAY CARE MOTHER

Many local councils license women to look after the children of working parents in the carer's own home. In areas with a lot of working mothers, the demand for day care is high and councils are anxious to recruit responsible women who can offer a safe, loving environment for children during the day. Contact your local council.

MARKET RESEARCH

Market research companies often need panels of respondents — in other words people who can answer questions about buying habits and attitudes to products. Sometimes they test advertisements by showing them to a group of respondents and studying their reactions. Strictly speaking this isn't home-based work — it involves either going to the market research office or sometimes a local venue arranged by the company. However, your time is paid for. A market researcher may contact you only once every few months, so the more companies you're listed with the better. You'll find the names of market research companies in the Yellow Pages.

HOLD A GARAGE SALE

A one-off moneymaker which helps you banish clutter at a profit. Some guidelines before you start:
● Publicise the event as much as you can with a small advertisement in the local classifieds, an eye-catching ad on community notice-boards, a sign festooned with balloons outside your house and, if possible, a sign at a major road or intersection with directions on how to find you.
● Hold it at the weekend and make it an early start, like 8am — 50 per cent of garage sale patrons are secondhand dealers who need to be in their shops by 10am.
● Know what sells well. Best sellers include old china, bric-a-brac, paperbacks, furniture, clothes.
● Sell as cheaply as possible — unless your prices are below those of secondhand shops, people may resist buying — and be prepared to slash prices come midday.

Cake decorating can be rewarding. A Melbourne woman who began by supplying friends and neighbours with delicious, beautifully-iced cakes, expanded her business by utilising the inexpensive services of an apprentice pastry cook and a student of icing techniques. She taught a neighbour how to perfect icing sugar roses. It became such a successful business that she sold to a larger operation.

Novelty cakes

DINOSAUR

2 packets buttercake mix
1 green Lifesaver (for eye)
licorice
200g pkt spearmint leaves (sweets)
white Tic Tacs
VIENNA CREAM
125g (4 oz) butter
1½ cups icing sugar
2 tablespoons milk
green food colouring

Make up cakes according to directions on packet, spread into two greased 28cm x 18cm (11in x 7in) lamington pans, bake in moderate oven 30 minutes, cool cakes on wire racks.

Cut out paper pattern using picture as a guide. Invert cakes on to flat surface, place pattern in position, cut around pattern with small serrated knife. See **above.**

Assemble dinosaur on prepared

Make up cake according to directions on packet, drop rounded teaspoonfuls of mixture into greased gem irons (see note at end), bake in moderate oven about 15 minutes, or until cakes are just beginning to shrink slightly, turn on to wire rack to cool.

This mixture will make about 50 to 60 cakes. (Cake mixture can stand at room temperature while the cakes are being cooked.)

To make necklace: Join cakes with a little of the cream to make the thickest part of the necklace; use small cutters to cut cakes smaller to represent graduating beads. Spread cakes with cream, roll in non-pareils. Thread cakes and sweets on to pipe cleaners. Decorate, using photograph below as a guide.

To make ring: Use a circular scrap of cake for "band", and a smaller piece of cake to represent the "stone"; spread both thinly with Cream; decorate.

To make earrings: Join cakes with a little Cream, spread more Cream on outside, roll in non-pareils or hundreds and thousands; decorate, using photograph below as a guide.

To make watch: Join two cakes with a little Cream, coat thinly with more Cream, roll in non-pareils; use cachous for figures on face of watch, use finely cut licorice for hands of watch, and licorice for strap. A thin slice of a licorice allsort is used for watch clasp.

See recipe for Vienna Cream at left, this page.

Note: Gem irons are available from hardware and cookware shops; if desired, round-based patty pans can be used instead, to make cakes. These larger cakes can be trimmed down to make "jewellery".

One packet mix will make about 36 of these larger cakes.

board, see **above**; join pieces with a little Vienna Cream. Spread top and sides of dinosaur with the Cream. Decorate body with halved spearmint leaves and other sweets, as shown. Use Tic Tacs, cut in half, for teeth; small pieces of licorice, cut into diamond shapes, for claws. Use thin strip of licorice to indicate upper jaws, above teeth; use a green Lifesaver for eye, then cut a small piece of licorice to make a pupil for the eye.

VIENNA CREAM

Have butter and milk at room temperature. Place butter in small bowl of electric mixer, beat until butter is as white as possible; gradually add about half the sifted icing sugar, beating constantly. Add milk gradually, then gradually beat in the remaining icing sugar. Mixture should be smooth and easy to spread with a spatula. Beat in few drops of green food colouring.

Note: Board for assembling dinosaur should be 60cm (24in) square.

EDIBLE "JEWELLERY"

This decorative array of edible "jewellery": — necklace, earrings, watch, ring — can have the required number of candles inserted into the small cakes for a birthday.

1 packet buttercake mix
assorted sweets
hundreds and thousands
non-pareils
cachous
licorice
pipe cleaners
VIENNA CREAM
185g (6oz) butter
2¼ cups icing sugar
3 tablespoons milk

Gardening

Garlanded with bougainvillaea and ivy, this tiny Sydney garden, **above**, is deceptively low maintenance; the plants chosen are hardy and need little pampering. No garden at all? The owner of this terrace house in North Sydney built a roof garden, **left**. Potted ferns and flowering plants are decor for alfresco parties. Not even a balcony, **right**, but an indoor garden in an inner-city loft. Pots of blooms are seasonal. Fixtures are ficus benjamina, kentia palms, spathiphyllum. **Far right**: the popular African violet.

50 PROBLEM SOLVERS FOR BUSY PEOPLE

For many of us today, time's too short for lovely big gardens with brilliant displays of annuals, perfect edges, manicured lawns. Low-care plots can still provide delicious havens for pottering. Easy-going gardener Don Burke gives some short cuts . . .

Indoor plants

1. Buy a few cheap indoor plants to cut your teeth on (Devil's ivy is number one best indoor plant because it's impossible to kill. Any philodendron is useful, and parlour palms and draecaenia margineta are extra hardy), but then stick with one or two large plants. That is, avoid a gaggle of tiny indoor pots; they need lots of maintenance yet never look spectacular in a room.

2. Other indoor survivors: Chinese happy plants, mother-in-law's tongue, madonna lilies (spathiphyllums) and aspidistras, once out of fashion, but gaining favour.

3. Always grow ferns in self-watering pots. The Decor Waterwell grows maidenhair to perfection and is reasonably cheap. Ferns have poor circulation so drying out does them massive damage and must be avoided.

4. Don't believe what you read on fertiliser labels. Most indoor plants only need fertilising once or twice a year — if that! Regular fertilising has been proven to kill indoor plants — so give it a miss.

5. African violets often get quite dusty since their leaves are hairy. Wash the entire plant in tepid water under the shower — but stand it to dry **out of the sun**. Never overwater. If an African violet doesn't re-flower within three months, place it carefully in the garbage bin — or move it to a new, brighter room where it will be happier.

A kentia palm and fishbone ferns are a luxuriant alternative to flowers, **right**. Clever idea for mobility, casters under a heavy pot, **below**. Windowsill potplants substitute for curtains.

6. Most indoor plant pots that look good don't drain, nor do they actually work properly. Conversely, most functional pots look awful. Buy any large, dramatic pots which suit your decor (normally ceramic or cane), then place your indoor plant inside it, still in its own nursery pot. Put a saucer inside the ceramic pot, of an appropriate size to collect the water draining from the nursery pot. Dress the top with coconut fibre to hide the inner pot. If the plant becomes a bit ratty after some months, swap another plant into the ceramic pot. It takes about 30 seconds!

7. Going away for a week or two? To water your indoor plants automatically: fill some plastic drink bottles with water and make a small hole in the bottom with a hot pin (or whatever). The very slow dripping from the bottle will water your plants for days.

8. Never put indoor plants out in full sun. Indoor plants have lost their "sun tan" and will burn badly if in the sun for even an hour.

9. Plants in hanging baskets are high maintenance plants because they dry out so rapidly. Also, since they hang close to the ceiling indoors, they get little direct sun and may not grow well. The ideal position for a hanging plant indoors is underneath a skylight, or lower down on a stand near a window.

10. If you can't spare the time to check when your indoor plants need watering — try the new Water Signals from Yates. These little poke-in labels change colour when they dry out.

11. To pot a plant:
(i) don't add drainage material in the bottom.
(ii) do put plastic flywire over large drain holes (if there are any).
(iii) do leave 3cm between top of potting mix and top of pot to help when watering.
(iv) do use commercial potting mix.
(v) do fertilise immediately with either Osmocote, Nutricote or Nitrosol.
(vi) do add Wetta Soil or Aqua Soil Wetter to help water penetration.

PLANT DIPLOMACY
Like people, some plants don't get along with others.
Antagonistic neighbours include strawberries and cabbages or their close relatives broccoli and cauliflowers. These don't do well as bed fellows. Onions and garlic tend to inhibit beans; on the other hand, they are compatible with beetroot, cucumbers, carrots and celery. Plant basil among tomatoes to help repel some pests.

Balcony gardens

12. Most balcony gardens come to grief because the pots are too small. Small pots dry out in a matter of hours on a hot, windy balcony. Put a huge tub or trough in one corner and fill it with lush foliage plants — flowering plants usually won't perform well on a balcony. Good plants are N.Z. Christmas bush, green coprosma, N.Z. cordyline or N.Z. flax.

13. There are also balcony vegies. For the life of me, I cannot imagine why you would bother to grow common vegies on a balcony. But there are delicious odd-ball varieties which are worth the effort. Try squat carrots, yellow zucchinis, the tiny yellow pear-shaped tomatoes, even snow peas, sugar snap peas or asparagus peas (all peas which you eat pod and all — grow them up a trellis or mesh). Grow the same way as herbs, but don't over-fertilise, especially carrots.

14. Most plants in hanging baskets will die on a balcony. Stick to ferociously hardy plants such as ivy geraniums, jasmine or asparagus "ferns" — and grow them in large baskets with an inner lining of alfoil or black plastic (with a hole in the bottom for drainage).

*Mini-care hanging baskets are ivy geraniums, **top**, in a variety of colours. Coloured pots give a lively focal point above a garage door. **Above**: pear tomatoes, snow peas, sugar snap peas. On a wrought-iron balcony, **below**, vivid bougainvillaea spills dramatically.*

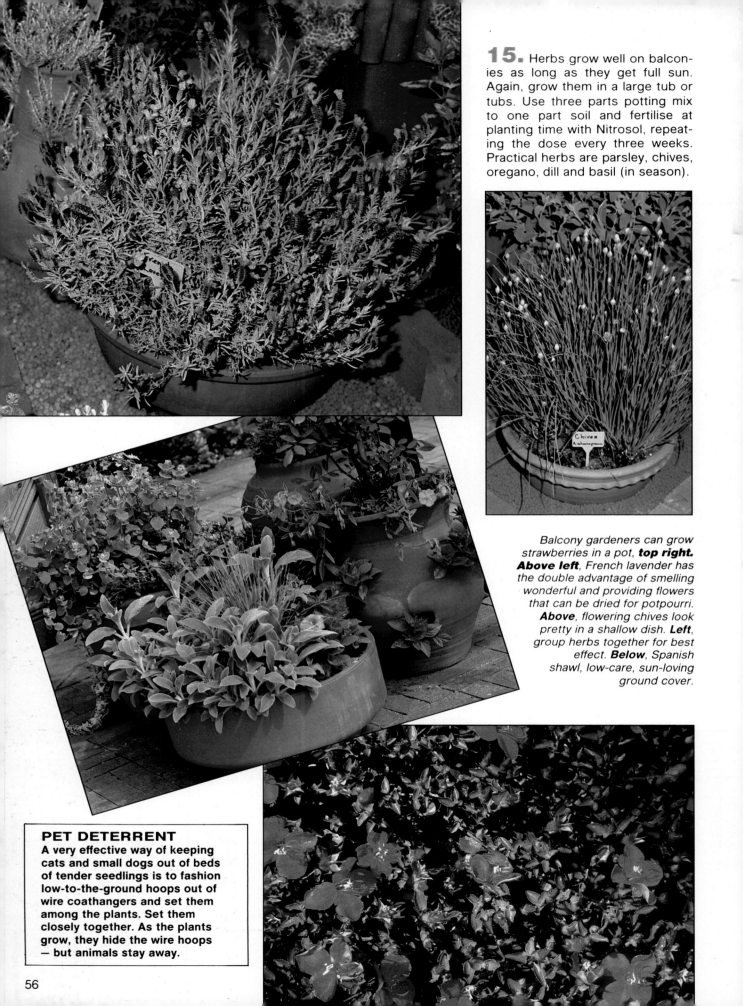

15. Herbs grow well on balconies as long as they get full sun. Again, grow them in a large tub or tubs. Use three parts potting mix to one part soil and fertilise at planting time with Nitrosol, repeating the dose every three weeks. Practical herbs are parsley, chives, oregano, dill and basil (in season).

Balcony gardeners can grow strawberries in a pot, *top right*. *Above left*, French lavender has the double advantage of smelling wonderful and providing flowers that can be dried for potpourri. *Above*, flowering chives look pretty in a shallow dish. *Left*, group herbs together for best effect. *Below*, Spanish shawl, low-care, sun-loving ground cover.

PET DETERRENT
A very effective way of keeping cats and small dogs out of beds of tender seedlings is to fashion low-to-the-ground hoops out of wire coathangers and set them among the plants. Set them closely together. As the plants grow, they hide the wire hoops — but animals stay away.

Money savers

16. Before you buy bags of pinebark mulch or potting mix, remember that many landscape supply companies or soil suppliers sell these items in bulk. You can take a trailer around on a Saturday morning and fill up for a fraction the price of bagged materials.

17. Low-maintenance gardens are essential for busy people, so consider paving with bricks or the new concrete pavers. Or establish hardy green ground cover in a shady area with native violet (viola hederacea) or kidney weed (dichondra). Sun-loving ground cover Spanish shawl (heterocentron elegans) makes a colourful show.

18. Strawberries are one of the best home fruits but only ever buy certified virus-free plants and replace them every two to three years. Aphids and other insects often carry a virus disease which saps vitality from the strawberries, lessening their production.

19. If you use plastic clip-on hose fittings, try to keep them out of the sun and away from loose dirt. Sun shortens the life of plastic fittings and grit will impede the clip release or fastening actions.

20. Never leave your garden tools out in the sun and rain. Always store them inside, they will last longer. Sharpen spades, secateurs, as necessary — it makes using them far easier.

Topiary trees in pots create pleasing formality in small gardens; they give perspective and focus the eye. Slow growers, they take years to shape and establish but once mature, require manicuring only once or twice a year during the growing season. Annie Wilkes of the Parterre Garden, Woollahra, NSW, specialises in topiary so that you can buy mature trees. *Top*, three-ball podacarpus give importance to backyard steps. *Above*, front entrance flanked by English box (buxus) topiaries; hardy mondo grass grows in base of centre pot. *Right*, shaped ivy, box tree topiary, paving and antique edging keep this inner city garden neat and fuss-free. It creates an 'outside room' which can be dressed up with potted flowers.

Time savers

21. When installing a new garden or a new garden area, think about some super-advanced or semi-mature shrubs or trees. These extra large plants cost around $25-$100 each but will create an "instant garden". It is possible to get a tree one to two metres high and just a few of these will create a stunning effect. The rest of the new garden can be ordinary sized plants.

22. Save time by **avoiding** disaster. If all your plants either die in the winter frost or burn in summer, adopt the old "walk around the block trick". Look for attractive plants in neighbourhood gardens — you'll have a good indication of

what grows well in your area. Pop in and ask the name of the plants; if they can't be identified, ask to snip off a piece to take to the local nursery for indentification.

23. Native shrubs and trees usually grow better and faster in smaller-sized pots. The 15cm (150mm) pots or smaller "tubes" are far cheaper yet produce bigger plants faster since their growth is not checked. Specialist native nurseries or Forestry Commissions are the best sources for natives.

*Passageway of an inner-city house, **above**, is clothed with ivy, hydrangea bushes, hanging and potted plants. **Right**, shady retreat is a mini-care summertime delight. The pink balsam (impatiens) takes care of itself.*

Problem-solvers for backyards that bake in the summer sun are cacti and some other succulents. The garden **at left** took months to establish but now delights its owners with interesting shapes and the intriguing flowers produced. Cacti can stand long periods of dryness because they have their own built-in water supply. Most desert cacti need bright to very bright light; those covered with spines or hairs thrive in direct sunlight. They do, however, appreciate modest watering.

Above: dahlias and phlox.
Top right: rose; below right: daffodils.

Fertilising

24. Fertilisers are not plant "foods" (despite fertiliser packet claims); plants feed on sugars which they make from sunshine. So, if your plant becomes sick, try giving it a feed — of extra sunlight!

25. Some plants will not perform well in the garden without fertilisers: citrus, vegies and annuals, roses, hibiscus, grass and fuchsias in particular. Others don't need much in the way of fertilisers at all: azaleas, native plants and proteas for instance. All pot plants **do** need fertilising: for pots and those plants which need little fertiliser stick to the nine-month release Osmocote or Nutricote.

26. Do fertilise your lawn once or twice a year with Complete Lawn Food. If you use sulphate of ammonia, you will need to re-treat the lawn in a few short weeks.

SHORT-CUT WHEN-TO-PLANT GUIDE

JANUARY	FEBRUARY	MARCH	APRIL	MAY	JUNE
petunias	violas	snapdragons	alyssum	camellias	roses
marigolds	cinerarias	carpeting sweet pea	livingstone daisies	flowering quinces	dianthus
salvia	primulas	— Snoopea	calendulas	luculia	lobelia
ageratum	pansies	sweet peas	dianthus	many types of grevilleas	calendulas
delphiniums		poppies	violas	violas	alyssum
poppies		stocks	pansies	pansies	English daisies
		pansies	anemones	alyssum	violas
	VEGETABLES	violas	primulas	Livingstone daisies	
	snow peas		ranunculus	lobelia	
VEGETABLES	Chinese cabbage		poppies	English daisies	
beans	sugar snap peas	**VEGETABLES**	stocks	calendulas	**VEGETABLES**
beetroot	broccoli	Brussels sprouts	sweet peas	dianthus	strawberries
Brussels sprouts	beans	beetroot	snapdragons	anemones	lettuce
(not in the tropics)	peas	Chinese cabbage	larkspurs	primulas	rhubarb
broccoli	carrots	peas	cornflowers	ranunculus	
cauliflower	beetroot	cauliflower	foxgloves	poppies	
cucumbers	cauliflower	cabbages	cinerarias	stocks	
cabbages	tomatoes (in	lettuce	(in the shade)	sweet peas	
carrots	warmer areas)	snow peas		snapdragons	
silver beet		silver beet		larkspurs	
radishes		parsley		cornflowers	
spring onions		radishes	**VEGETABLES**		
sweet corn		carrots	cabbages		
zucchinis			onions	**VEGETABLES**	
			peas	cauliflower	
			snow peas	lettuce	
			Chinese cabbage	radishes	
			lettuce	spinach	
			radishes	broad beans (not in	
			spinach	the tropics)	

Knowing what to plant at what time of the year is a definite money-saver for busy gardeners; you cut down on failures and eliminate seasons of haphazard experimentation. This is a general guide to growing annuals and vegetables throughout Australia. Whilst there may be minor regional variations, these have been chosen because they can be grown successfully almost anywhere in Australia at the time designated.

Pests

27. Mealy-bugs (white, furry, match-head sized insects) on indoor plants are very difficult to control. Many books say to dab with methylated spirits but this will not solve the problem. Take the plant outside and spray with Lebaycid — repeat spraying in two weeks.

28. Small, black flying insects on and around your indoor plants do no harm. Spray if you must with an aerosol such as Mortein House and Garden, but more flies will return in a day or so.

29. Caterpillars on large gum trees rarely damage the tree significantly — so live and let live. Severe, repeated attacks can be treated by tree injection with an appropriate insecticide. Ask your local Forestry Department about this.

30. If your trees are damaged by borers or dieback: cut off all dead material, taking care to leave clean non-jagged wounds. Then fertilise and water the tree and leave it to repair itself. Toxic chemicals or tree paints on borer holes are of dubious value.

31. To kill snails, place snail baits inside terra cotta pipes — the snails still crawl in to get the baits, but it prevents dogs from eating the baits and being poisoned.

32. Never try to get rid of oxalis and onion-weed by digging them out. This merely spreads them. Spot treat with Zero or Roundup. Follow-up treatments are required, but eventually you will win!

JULY	AUGUST	SEPTEMBER	OCTOBER	NOVEMBER	DECEMBER
gladioli (in warmer regions)	fuchsias	best of the annuals:	petunias	plant annuals in hanging baskets:	petunias
alyssum	azaleas	petunias	marigolds	blue and white petunias	marigolds
calendulas	shasta daisies	marigolds	phlox	alyssum	phlox
candytuft	camellias	dwarf blue ageratum	ageratum	marigolds	ageratum
delphiniums	pigface	bedding begonias	alyssum	phlox	alyssum
dianthus	gladioli		dahlias	dahlias	salvia
gypsophila	citrus		salvias	salvia	
larkspurs	perennial phlox	**VEGETABLES**	hibiscus		
lupins	perennial asters	beetroot	bougainvilleas		**VEGETABLES**
Virginia stocks	rhododendrons	cabbages		**VEGETABLES**	tomatoes
	callas	capsicums		tomatoes	beans
		carrots	**VEGETABLES**	Chinese cabbage	zucchinis
		lettuce	tomatoes (cocktail	beans	radishes
VEGETABLES		spring onions	fruiting varieties	cucumbers	pumpkins
broad beans	**VEGETABLES**	parsnips	eg. Tiny Tim)	zucchinis	cucumbers
potatoes	peas	radishes	silver beet	pumpkins	beetroot
peas	potatoes	peas	capsicums	radishes	lettuce
cabbages	carrots	rhubarb	cabbages	beetroot	silver beet
carrots	herbs	silver beet	carrots	silver beet	celery
lettuce	lettuce	herbs:	lettuce	lettuce	herbs
onions	radishes	chives	celery	celery	corn
radishes	silver beet	mint	beetroot	capsicums	
rhubarb	beetroot	parsley	radishes	carrots	
shallots		rosemary	pumpkins	cabbages	
spinach		thyme	zucchinis	herbs.	
		oregano	beans	May be too late	
			cucumbers	for cabbages and	
			herbs:	carrots in tropical zones.	
			marjoram		
			parsley		
			thyme		
			basil		
			mint		

Sprays

33. You wouldn't buy medicine from anyone but a chemist and you should never buy garden pesticides from untrained people. You are within your rights to ask to speak to a qualified horticulturist at your local nursery when selecting chemicals. Do so, because these people are experienced in this.

34. Never buy loads of different sprays for the garden. Consult a horticulturist and select a very small number of sprays. Make sure that you know what they do and how dangerous they are. Real dangers occur when you are confused about your sprays.

35. Store all garden pesticides in a cupboard (preferably locked) well up out of reach of kids and pets. Dogs love snail bait, but it can easily kill them. ''Deadline'' snail bait claims to repel dogs and cats, so may be safer.

36. Most poisonings of kids occur when stupid people store garden pesticides in softdrink bottles. This is illegal and dangerous.

37. When spraying anything, stop immediately if you get any spray drift or spillage on your skin (especially face and eyes). Go inside, wash with soap and then return to finish the spraying. **Never** smoke or eat while spraying.

38. Don't use ''alternate'' sprays such as garlic. These sprays don't work as well as or as long as normal pesticides; you finish up spraying two or three times as often. Pyrethrin sprays are very low in toxicity, safe and really do work.

39. Most garden sprays work better if you add a few drops of dishwashing liquid to the spray mix. This lessens the surface tension of the water and enables it to both spread and penetrate well.

> **PLANT SHELTERS**
> To shade newly-planted seedlings on hot days, cut large plastic icecream containers in halves or quarters, then place them over the small plants with the covered-in part facing north.

*Quick and easy way to fix leaks in fish ponds, such as the one **below**: mix one part of Silasec, one part of Bondcrete, six parts of cement powder and five parts water. Brush three coats well into the pond walls, neutralise cement with vinegar or alum then refill pond. If large cracks are present, first fill them with an exterior waterproof mastic, then paint as above.*

Mulching

40. Leaving a bare soil surface is both unnatural and unwise; it causes weeds to grow, which in turn leads to excessive soil disturbance as the weeds are removed. Cover all bare soils with a 75mm (eight cm) thick layer of pinebark, shredded wood, compost or leaf litter.

41. In areas of excessive weed growth, lay newspaper down under the mulch to further inhibit weeds; four to six sheet thickness will do, but never use black plastic since it damages both soil and plants.

42. Thick mulches around azaleas and rhododendrons do more harm than good. Between 25-40mm (three to five cm) is thick enough. After a year or two natural leaf fall will do the job for you.

*Never attach staghorns or elkhorns to trees; nail or tie them to a board first. The thriving specimen, **right**, is nailed to a board in a shadehouse.*

Even if you have a large garden, try growing the hardy, cheerful geranium, *above*, in containers. You can move pots around to add extra colour, use them as al fresco table centrepieces, or bring them inside. As a money-saving measure, grow several so that you can give well-established plants on birthdays or at Christmas as gifts.

Drainage

43. The most common garden mistake is that of ruining the natural drainage of the block of land, leading to boggy spots and flooding. Virgin land always has ways of shedding water: gentle contours, through to creeks all dispense water when it rains. Most gardens are artificially levelled, leaving the busy homeowner with constant water problems. Consider gently contouring your lawn and gardens to shed water. Very slight depressions can collect and move away vast amounts of water — far more than any agricultural drain.

44. Mossy lawns are caused by too much water, too little light and alkaline conditions. Mix four tablespoons of iron sulphate into a watering can of water and apply to bad spots. Better still, remove the lawn and replace with shade tolerant groundcovers — native violet, dichondra, or turn the area into a garden full of balsam and ferns.

Other tips

45. Staghorn and elkhorn ferns look great attached to trees but they may do the poor tree lots of harm. Never attach them directly to a tree. Nail or tie them to a board and then nail the board on to the tree. Never, under any circumstances, tie anything to a tree. Wire or rope will cut into the trunk as the tree grows in girth and this will seriously damage, or even kill.

46. Where possible, don't artificially feed native birds — this may upset the birds and the local ecology. Feed birds by planting a variety of wonderful native plants such as grevilleas, banksias, kangaroo paws or bottlebrush.

47. Staking plants may not help them at all. Staking leads to weakened, spindly growth and the tree or shrub may possibly fall over when it outgrows the stake. On windy sites, plant smaller pot sizes of plants. Never tie tightly to one stake — always strap loosely to two or three stakes with hessian straps or nylon stocking.

48. To strike cuttings, put 10-20 10cm cuttings into a 15cm pot filled with a 50/50 sand, peat mix. Dip cuttings in rooting hormone and water pot well. Then enclose in a clear plastic bag, tie top and place in shady area for four to six weeks. Hopefully some will sprout.

49. Gardeners worry too much about the exact time to prune. The time to prune is when **you** have time. So long as you understand that if you prune before flowering you will lessen the number of flowers — but so what. Severe pruning of plants in summer can result in sunburn of branches and trunk; light pruning is okay. This rule applies for all plants and trees. Main thing to remember: sharp secateurs and clean cuts.

50. If your native boronia, daphne, waratah and other 'touchy' plants shrivel up and die the minute you plant them in the garden, install them in pots. Buy a good commercial potting mix and treat the plant's root ball with Fongarid to stop root rot. Most touchy plants grow well in large tubs.

Découpage

DECORATING WITH PAPER CUT OUTS

To create a design or decoration, different patterns and motifs are taken from various papers and glued onto the article to be adorned, then varnished.

Above, geometric paper cut outs dramatise a pair of plain black plastic earrings. **Below**, previously varnished door handles have been given a new look with simple floral cut outs. Both items are varnished afterwards.

Wooden waste paper bin, *above and left*, was prepared in same way as wooden boxes on next page. First, black household oil paint was used to paint box. The gold lines are paper self adhesive. Twenty-three coats of varnish were applied, then rubbed back and polished.

The word Découpage is derived from the French verb "découper" — to cut out; it is the ancient art of decorating with paper cut outs. While its earliest origins are uncertain, there are fascinating examples of découpage from China and Persia dating back to approximately 1400AD. The art of découpage is relatively simple. It is an inexpensive pastime, requiring only patience, time and an appreciation of colour and design. It is particularly rewarding for those who may not be able to draw or paint but who wish to create a thing of beauty. Wrapping paper, cards, calendars, old prints and books may be cut up to decorate a variety of objects from a thimble to a piece of furniture. Any smooth surface such as wood, glass, porcelain, shells or silk fabric may be enhanced. Audrey Raymond of The Découpage Studio, Sydney, shows some popular and easily achieved découpage decoration.

Above, porcelain pot was decorated with delicate card cut outs and varnished.

Découpage as it is known today had its roots in late 17th century Italy and blossomed throughout Europe in the 18th century. When Oriental lacquered furniture and objets d'art came into vogue, Venetian cabinet makers used hand-coloured engravings and prints which they cut out and pasted onto furniture and wall panels to decorate them in the Oriental style. These were then covered with many layers of lacquer to give the impression they were handpainted.

From Italy this practice spread throughout Europe and in the French court of Louis XVI, young men visiting ladies in the court brought them gifts of original drawings and prints to cut up while they sat in their salons.

It became a very popular pastime in Victorian England when ladies used embossed papers, valentine and greeting cards, postcards and magazine cuttings to decorate tabletops, boxes, trays and screens.

By the beginning of this century the enthusiasm for découpage had waned, but a small group in the United States kept it alive and formed the National Guild of Découpeurs in 1971.

The objects for découpage must be sanded smooth with all holes and blemishes filled and painted or stained before pasting can begin. After pasting on cut outs, about 25 layers of varnish are applied with occasional wet sanding to remove dust and imperfections. After a final sanding the article is polished with quality wax or furniture polish.

Small cuticle scissors (preferably curved) are the most suitable for cutting and paper should be kept thin. With practise, cutting becomes easier and more delicate; many people find snipping away with a pair of scissors therapeutic.

Apart from the traditional découpage under layers of varnish, there are many other forms of this fascinating art. Elevation is the name given to three dimensional pictures and decorative design; repoussé is when the paper is moulded and padded from underneath. Découpage may be applied under glass and it takes on the appearance of decorated porcelain. Many background finishes may be used such as gold leaf, mother-of-pearl inlay or tortoiseshell finish.

Materials: wet and dry sandpaper (numbers 400, 600, 1000) or 220 garnet for rough woods, fast drying acrylic paints or household oil paints; scalpel or x-acto knife with very fine point, cuticle scissors with short fine blade (preferably curved), fine pointed tweezers for handling cut outs, blu-tack adhesive, tack cloth, small natural sponge, wax paper, Aquadhere glue or cellulose wallpaper paste, coloured pencils (not watercolour) to touch up prints, paint brushes, wrapping paper, illustrations, acrylic sealer, wood putty, varnish (eg: Estapol or Watsonia Satin Proof), household turps. We used a small wooden pine box in the example demonstrated below.

Wooden box

Materials: small wooden pine box, sandpaper (400, 600 and 1000 wet/dry), wrapping paper, cards, old prints, coloured pencils, acrylic sealer, cuticule scissors, tweezers, blu-tack, Aquadhere, sponge, white shellac (if this is unavailable, apply three to four coats of Gesso, dry sanding between coats and wet sanding the last coat to a porcelain finish), wood putty, varnish, wax paper, tack cloth.

1. Sand box smooth with **dry** 400 wet/dry sandpaper. Fill any holes or stubborn grain marks with wood putty. Sand back putty, when surface is smooth, seal box with a coat of white shellac.

2. Select wrapping paper or cards with which to decorate box. Paper should not be too thick or have printing on the back. We used Italian Florentine wrapping paper.

3. Before cutting paper, thicken any fine lines with a coloured pencil. Spray face of the print with acrylic sealer to strengthen paper and seal colour.

4. Cut paper with curve of cuticle scissors pointing outwards. (Tiny areas can be cut with a scalpel). When prints are cut, colour the white edges with a pencil or paint (don't use watercolour).

A beautiful piece of découpage is one which is perfectly smooth so the paper cannot be detected.

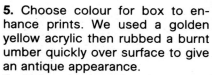

5. Choose colour for box to enhance prints. We used a golden yellow acrylic then rubbed a burnt umber quickly over surface to give an antique appearance.

6. Using tweezers, arrange cut outs into a design on box. Keep lines flowing and objects in proportion — don't have a butterfly larger than a bird. Hold the cut outs in place with blu-tack.

7. Working on a piece of wax paper, apply Aquadhere glue to back of cut outs and stick onto box. Always keep a damp (not wet) natural sponge handy to press down cut out then clean up excess glue. Cut outs can be placed over the lid join and sliced with a scalpel before varnishing the box.

Between each stage,
wipe box with tack
cloth to remove dust.

8. Thoroughly clean box with a damp sponge and check that all edges are glued down by running around them with a toothpick before varnishing.

9. Apply long strokes of varnish with a paint brush. Some varnishes have a strong yellowing effect which mellows and dulls colours slightly. A water-based varnish, if available, dries more quickly. Do not apply varnish too thickly, avoid drips and runs. Apply alternate coats in opposite directions. Keep box in dust-free environment.

10. After about 10 coats, sand lightly with **wet** 400 sandpaper to remove dust and bubbles. Continue to wet sand every three coats, making sure the varnish is dry (about 6 hours) before applying the next coat. Around the 20th coat change to 600 wet/dry sandpaper. When you have a smooth surface and cannot feel the paper (from about the 25th coat onwards) you can give a final sanding of 1000 wet/dry. Wet sand until there are no shiny areas; it is all dull. Finish with furniture polish or beeswax.

Lampstand

Materials: hollow cylindrical lamp (hurricane lamp), oil paint, cellulose wallpaper paste, natural sponge, cotton buds, tooth picks, methylated spirits.

1. A cellulose wallpaper paste should be used to stick prints to glass. Place paste on face of print and press onto glass. Press print down with damp fingers and sponge. Clean glass as much as possible, then gently press out air bubbles that appear as shiny spots. Never spray face of prints or use shiny paper prints for découpage under glass.

2. Check edges are stuck down and clean glass with cotton buds and toothpicks dipped in methylated spirits or vinegar and water.

3. Apply an oil-based paint behind cut outs and onto glass. Try not to use an acrylic paint as it may crack with time.

Prints are applied from within, under the glass. White artists' oil paint has been smeared on with the fingers, to give the appearance of porcelain.

Audrey Raymond of The Découpage Studio can be contacted at P.O. Box C438 Clarence St, Sydney 2000, or on (02) 387 6029.

Spectacle lenses, *below*, have been mounted and framed after being découpaged as under glass: simple, quick, highly effective découpage.

Left, silk lampshade has been decorated with paper cut outs which have been glued on. There is no need to varnish the lampshade. *Below*, clear glass plate takes on a fantasy look with the addition of fairies which have been glued on the back of plate. White paint has been applied over them.

Brighten up a door with the colourful finger plate, **left**. Australian birds were cut out and pasted onto the back of the glass plate; pale green paint was then applied behind the cut outs. A clear glass plate, **above**, becomes a showpiece with the addition of Japanese sashes cut from wrapping paper and glued to the back of the plate. Patterned rice paper was then glued over the sashes and trimmed around the plate edges. Three coats of varnish behind the plate made it useable. **Below**, the two Oriental-style trivets have had gold leaf applied instead of paint. The one **at left** is used with asphaltum to give a tortoiseshell effect. The small glass box also has a gold leaf background. The paperweight was backed with sprinkled gold powder under blue artists' oil paint.

Hand coloured black and white pictures were stuck onto gold paper and then cut out to give a defining gold line around the prints on the wooden bottle, *left*. The bowl was stippled with blue and green oil paints. Pencils (not watercolour ones) are used to hand colour prints. The technique gives the appearance of fine cloisonné ware.

*A shabby side table gets a new lease on life with a more contemporary style of découpage, **above, below, right**. The table was firstly painted with a matt finish white paint. Vividly coloured photographs with the theme of make-up were cut from various magazines and positioned on the table. Then began the task of pasting them on in their designated positions, varnishing and sanding. It is the same process as the wooden boxes on page 66. Try not to paste layer upon layer as the heavy build up will make it necessary to add many extra coats of varnish. It is a time consuming process as you must wait for one coat of varnish to dry before applying the next.*

*Easy-to-do framed picture, **above**. A small bird has been glued onto the back of a brass frame and glass placed on top. **Above right**, round wooden tray was sprayed with black gloss paint, decorated with paper prints and varnished.*

Pizazz with Paint

SPATTER, SPONGE, STIPPLE AND OTHER FUN EFFECTS

A marvellous way to give familiar objects or furniture new interest is to apply a 'painted finish' using techniques that are easy — once you know how. You can achieve fine spatter or stipple effects, make patterns in paint with a chamois, create the illusion of cracked surfaces, or dab on designs with a sponge. Ceilings, walls, tables, chairs, boxes, lampshades are among the everyday things that can be transformed with paint, patience and quickly learned skills. Jennifer Bennell, who runs courses in these and more elaborate decorative techniques, shows some easily achieved finishes.

Left: spattering is simply a smattering of paint spots, on furniture or decorative objects. See page 74 for instructions. The photo also contains examples of chamois and sponge work.

Jennifer Bennell is author of Painted Illusions, a book covering these and many other painted finishes. Enquiries to The Painted Finish, 2 Paddington Street, Paddington, NSW. See page 128 for stockists.

PREPARATION

Surfaces to be 'finished' may be plastic (or similar), ceramic, enamel, smooth metal or wood. If the piece is raw, as in the case of unpainted wood, ceramic or metal, it must be prepared by sanding with no. 220 sandpaper (coarser if the surface is rough), then sealed with undercoat such as Pascol Enamel All-purpose Undercoat (other companies make similar). Allow to dry overnight, sand again, apply coat of thinned semi-gloss (satin) oil-based enamel. Dry 24 hours, sand again, apply second coat of semi-gloss. The piece is then ready to apply the antiquing glaze (see box, next page). Glass, plastic or glazed ceramic surfaces may have antiquing medium applied without preparation — however the finish may then chip more easily.

Decorating terracotta pots

Materials: pots; flat plastic water-based paint (dark green for base coat, also paler green, black and white); sea sponge (available from pharmacists) which has been dipped in water and carefully wrung out so that no water remains (this makes sponge malleable); gloss exterior varnish; turkey (or strong) feather.

1. Paint pot all over with quick-drying dark green flat plastic paint.
2. When dry, dab black paint, at random, all over quickly with sponge, leaving some areas lighter than others.
3. Apply more drifts over the black at random with paler green paint — not all over and not as densely as the black.
4. To apply veining, dip a long turkey feather into thinned white paint and drag edge of feather diagonally along pot from bottom to top. Position some veins on the edges of denser areas of the pattern. Place veins approximately at equal distances around pot; too few are better than too many **(see above)**.
5. Leave to dry, then varnish with two coats of varnish.
Note: Don't use pots with raised decorative edges or carved designs. A smooth surface works more successfully.

Spatter finish

Materials: fine surgical gloves; paint (thinned-down oil-based paint, fairly runny so that it may be applied easily; artists' oils, acrylics or any oil- or water-based house paint can be used); spatter brush (see how-to-make box); clean white paper to work on (newsprint comes off).

Load brush with paint and pull along the white paper on all sides to remove excess runny paint so that potential drips are avoided.

To achieve a spatter, turn flat brush sideways, **below**, and hold in left hand, put right thumb on top of metal base of brush and pull gloved forefinger up over end of bristles from bottom to top so paint sprays onto surface. If you get a drop of paint onto the surface, dab off with a cotton bud. Eventually the spatter concentration will cover the blemish. When finished, use another colour if you wish a two-colour effect, **below**. Use a different brush for each colour. Varnish.

HOW TO MAKE A SPATTER BRUSH. Buy an inexpensive medium-size flat bristle brush (approx 25mm). Wind masking tape around bristles 20mm from metal base and then tape around end of bristles. Cut through bristles using a meat cleaver and hammer, as shown.

Right: placemats before spatter treatment.

To create negative striping, first mask shape or design with graphic artists' border tape or Letraset tape. You then apply the chosen finish (example *below* is stippling) and remove border tape before paint has 'set up', or dried.

Left and above: other examples of spatter finish. Plain glass tumblers are now pretty vases.

Chamois finish

Materials: scumbling medium; japan or flat oil-based enamel; fresh chamois; stipple brush (or shaving brush); exterior varnish; turps; oxhair or nylon brush to paint on antiquing medium.

1. Mix one part paint, one part scumbling medium and half part turps to achieve antiquing medium, paint on, pounce with stipple brush to remove brush strokes (see next page for stipple finish).

2. Take rolled chamois (previously moistened in water and wrung out so that it is malleable and almost dry) and place it diagonally across the painted surface, leaving an imprint. Use a dabbing motion and press firmly (too firmly will leave fingerprints). It is essential to work quickly so that the surface paint has not begun to dry. Give at least two coats varnish.

Sponging

Materials: gloves; sea sponges; japan or flat oil-based enamels; turps; white paper to work on; scumbling medium; exterior varnish.

Mix the antiquing medium (one part paint, one part scumbling medium, one part turps), then dip sponge lightly into mixture, unload excess paint by pressing onto white paper, then lightly begin to dab sponge onto surface in an up-and-down motion. You create depth of colour by applying a heavier loading in some areas and lighter in others; this gives more shading and contrast. Do not allow sponge to move on surface; apply at random **(below)** so that no straight lines appear (the aim is to achieve a slightly marbled effect). Varnish.

Stipple finish

Materials: stipple brush (this is a thick pig bristle brush. A common stencilling brush will not do because of the conformation of the bristles — a stipple brush has a rounded head); japan or flat oil-based enamels; scumbling medium; turps; gloves; gloss exterior varnish; oxhair or nylon brush to paint on antiquing medium.

1. Mix antiquing medium (one part paint, one part scumbling medium, half part turps), quickly paint mixture onto surface (speed is important), then use stipple brush in an up-and-down motion to remove brush strokes.

2. Allow mixture to set up for an hour, then remove any previously applied masking tape. Leave 24 hours. Apply varnish, either gloss or satin (minimum of 2 gloss or 3 satin coats).

Strié (dragging)

Materials: soft ox-hair or nylon brush; paint; scumbling medium; turps; white paper; stiff bristle brush.

Mix antiquing medium (one part paint, one part scumbling medium, half part turps). Quickly paint on the antiquing medium, then take the stiff bristle brush in your right hand and pull backwards and forwards across the surface **(as below)** so that the paint is removed. After each stroke, quickly wipe the paint off the brush so that it is not redistributed on the surface. The brush should be pulled across the paint about three to four times. After this, the paint begins to set up (dry, so that it no longer holds the impression of the chamois) and will take on a bruised appearance if overworked. Varnish.

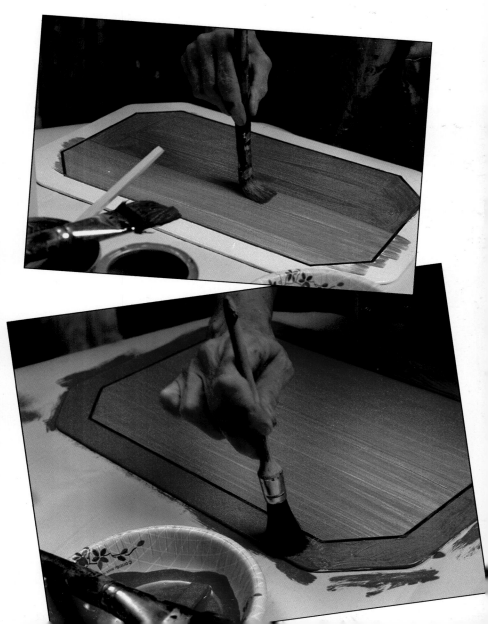

Crackle finish

Crackle work is great fun because the painting is almost slapdash. The more thickly applied, the stronger and more graphic the crackle design.

Materials: crackle medium (from The Painted Finish); any water-based house paint; two good quality nylon brushes; gloss varnish.

1. The crackle medium, which is thick and sticky, is painted onto the prepared surface and allowed to dry (about two hours). If the medium appears to have 'crawled' (looks lacy, with lots of holes) apply a second coat. The crawling seems to occur only on an already prepared surface such as this table **(pictured below right).**

2. When absolutely dry, apply paint. This must be water-based, otherwise the crack will not occur. On a large surface apply an extremely well-loaded brush with short criss-cross strokes. Do not draw the brush across a long surface in straight strokes as the paint quickly runs out and each re-loading will show up. The heavier the application, the more graphic the crack.

As the paint dries, cracking begins. Dry overnight. A finish of at least three coats of high gloss varnish is essential.

Note: The brush for the crackle medium must be washed in turps, hot water and detergent immediately after it has been used.

After using oil-based paints, wash brushes immediately in turps. If you ever have a problem with brushes hardening, boil a saucepan of water, detergent and ammonia and keep dipping the brush into boiling water until it becomes soft.

Tracing images

Tracings can be made from drawings, cartoons, even designs on fabrics, as shown on these pages.

Materials: tracing or greaseproof paper or artists' transfer paper (artists' carbon); hard pencil, 2H; greaseproof kitchen paper; japan paint or flat oil-based enamel, acrylics or artists' oils (drying time of these paints longer).

1. Trace figures on greaseproof or tracing paper.

2. Place transfer paper (which acts like carbon paper) between tracing paper and surface and trace very carefully.

3. Paint in images with acrylics; then apply at least three coats of high gloss varnish.

For stirring paint, Japanese wooden joined chopsticks (available most Asian speciality stores) are ideal.

*These intricate tracings, **below**, were applied to the top of an old sewing machine which had first been painted dark green. This same principle of tracing was applied to transfer a fabric design onto a bedroom sidetable, **above**, which was then carefully painted to match curtains and cushions in the room. The tracing technique was also used for the tray at **left**.*

PAPER STENCILLING

Stencilling is one of the simplest, least expensive and oldest forms of decoration. In colonial days, wallpaper was scarce so artists created the illusion with stencils. Surfaces to stencil include floors, walls, tiles, wooden surfaces (must be sealed or varnished), plastic or metal plates, trays or boxes, even fabrics. The paper stencilling exercises were created for us by Kevin Tenney, who teaches bronze powder stencilling, gilding, and other techniques at The Painted Finish, Sydney.

Note: Remember, in making your own stencil, the shape you're cutting away becomes the finished image that remains.

Stencilled patterns have given new character to the floor of a Sydney dining room, **below**. Not difficult to do, the patterns were achieved with hard-wearing acrylic paint. See guideline to the design, following pages. Use your own ideas and experiment. Stencilling can work wonders on a child's suitcase, **above**, or give new character to an inexpensive chest of drawers as seen **at left.**

Books of stencils are available from book shops. You can make your own stencils from oiled stencil paper, frosted acetate (drafting film) or manilla folders. The manilla folder must be oiled so the paint doesn't soak in. Use a mixture of half raw linseed oil to half turpentine. Wipe folder over and allow about 10 minutes to dry. Draw your design onto folder before it is oiled.

1. Draw a stencil design onto folder. Oil manilla folder and leave to dry. Frosted acetate or stencil paper need not be oiled.

2. Cut stencil out on cutting board or wad of newspapers. It is easier to move the paper as you cut rather than the blade; keep blade in one position.

3. Position stencil onto surface where design is to appear. Tape it firmly in place.

4. Pour paint into an old saucer.

5. Lightly dip stencil brush in paint.

6. On paper towel or newspaper, dab or strike the brush downwards until colour is evenly distributed through brush.

7. Apply colour to exposed area of stencil in a dabbing motion, build up colour gradually. Cover whole area first. Where you require a deeper colour, go back over the area. Different colours can be blended in.

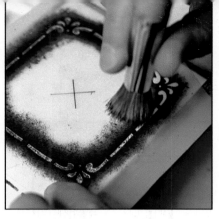

8. Use a different brush for each colour.

9. Remove stencil. If adding another section to the design, wait for paint to dry, repeat process.

10. When design is completed, allow it to dry and cover with varnish.

Materials: stencils (either bought or made from the materials mentioned), craft knife, single-edged razor blade or scalpel (needs to be very sharp and precise); japan craft enamel or any acrylic paint which dries quickly and doesn't run; stencil brushes (these have flat-topped bristles); varnish and paintbrush; masking tape.

Use bigger brushes for larger sized stencils with more area.

Bronze powder stencilling

In this more advanced process (example **above** and **below**), acrylic paints are replaced by bronze powders. Stencil brushes are not used and the stencil is made from architects' linen (a tracing cloth which will cut but still hold its shape because of its weave); frosted acetate can also be used.

The object to be stencilled is varnished. When varnish is almost dry, the stencil is placed in position. Different coloured bronze powders are placed in saucers, and the index finger is wrapped in a piece of velvet, leather or chamois. The finger is then dipped into powder and powder is rubbed onto the almost dry surface to form the specific stencil pattern.

Complexity lies in cutting the stencils. The application is quite simple; a well cut stencil is imperative to a good design.

Acetate is a good substance from which to make stencils because it is translucent. You can see where to place the second colour more accurately on the design.

One of the easiest patterns to stencil is a design of checks, **right.** They can be bold and dramatic or subtle and simple, and the design is timeless. Checks follow the rim of this inexpensive metal tray bought from a furniture store; a stencil of fruit has been added in the centre. Stencils with an Australiana theme were used to decorate the plain blue chest of drawers on these pages. It was originally a mass-produced whitewood chest to which a stippled paint finish was applied. Several stencils of the waratah, flannel flowers and leaves were cut separately and stencilled onto the chest, **below.**

Individual Flair
CLEVER DECORATING

It's surprising what effects you can achieve with simple kitchen items, a few treasured possessions, a splash of paint and lots of imagination. We've selected some wonderful decorating ideas from various people to show you how easy it can be to brighten a room and demonstrate unexpected individuality.

A collection of baskets of different shapes and sizes, **above**, teamed with a bunch of dried gum nuts and an old pitchfork provide an eyecatching display. The baskets hang on nails or are attached to the pitchfork with string. To match the blue and white theme of the kitchen, the owner created a cloud-like design on the ceiling, **right**. A sponge attached to a long stick was dipped in fast-drying acrylic paint, then dabbed onto the ceiling. Other colours were added as desired.

Wooden kitchen utensils, an enamel funnel and an iron scale clustered together with string give a rustic feel to a kitchen window, **right**. Coloured wooden animals line the sill and hang as a mobile for extra effect.

The rich tones of tapestry yarn in a simple basket, **left**, make a lovely decoration. A touch of colour is added inside with fresh potted flowers, **below**. An assortment of stuffed animals or well-loved toys in matching baskets enliven a quiet corner, **bottom**.

Look again at any peeling, worn-out garden furniture sitting around in the shed or garage: it can be transformed with bright new paint colours into an asset for inside the house, **left**.

Folk art cat

Materials: artists' acrylics, plywood shape (shape can also be fashioned from heavy cardboard).

This 'shelf cat' is an example of the growing interest in decorative painting in Australia. Monica Hall, of Pymble, NSW, runs classes in the art of "Bauernmalerei". She uses Jo Sonja's Artists' Colours (available through Chroma Acrylics (NSW) Pty Ltd) because they are very long wearing. Cat shapes are available from Monica Hall for $15, or they may be made from balsa wood or even heavy cardboard. Paint on daisies, pansies, forget-me-nots, and any flowers you fancy. The cat shape has a board protruding at a right angle from behind, so that it can sit on mantel, windowsill, bookcase or kitchen shelf.

Busy Hands

Even the busiest people may find time to make articles that end up as family heirlooms and keepsakes. Experts show how to create handcraft, from a counted cross-stitch frog and papier mâché jewellery to quilted cushions.

CROSS-STITCH TREE FROG

Children love identifying their room as their own, and this wonderful Red-eyed tree frog proclaims it! Rachel Dulson created the design for us, based on this colourful Australian frog.

Cross-stitch can be done on all fabrics which are even weave, and have threads that can be counted. The embroidery thread should be of a weight comparable to the chosen fabric. If the embroidery thread is too thick it can make the finished work look bulky, or if the thread is too thin the background fabric will show through. It is also important not to pull the stitches too tight; they should lie even and smooth.

YOUR STITCH GUIDE
A cross-stitch is comprised of an under-stitch and an over-stitch which are sewn, in this case, over one thread of the fabric.

Cross-stitches can be sewn in both horizontal and vertical rows.

If you are working the stitches horizontally, first sew the desired number of under-stitches from left to right then sew back from right to left with the over-stitches.

When sewing vertically, complete each stitch individually.

There are two important rules for cross-stitch work: 1. The under-stitches must always lie in the same direction diagonally, with the over-stitches sewn on the opposite diagonal. This is vital to ensure a smooth, good-looking piece of finished work. Stitches on the wrong side of the work are always vertical.
2. Never skip over more than the space of two stitches whether it be vertical or horizontal as the loose thread carried over the back of the work may become visible through the fabric.

THREAD
This embroidery can be sewn with either Danish Flower Thread, which we used, or with DMC stranded cotton.

If you choose the Danish Flower Thread, only one strand is used. The DMC, however, has to be split and two of the six strands used.

Materials: white Aida fabric (11 count) 25cm x 25cm; one skein, either Danish Flower Thread (DFT) or DMC of each colour indicated in the colour key; one size 24, blunt-ended embroidery needle; pair of embroidery scissors. All of these materials are available from craft shops.

Our Red-eyed tree frog was designed by Stitcheree Designs, producers of counted cross-stitch kits with Australian themes: PO Box 153, Double Bay, 2028, NSW.

GRAPH

Each symbol on the graph represents a different colour, as indicated on the colour key. When sewing this door plaque for your own child, plan name placement on graph paper before stitching.

HOW TO START

To prevent the fabric from fraying, over sew or machine sew around the edge. Once done, fold the fabric lengthways and tack a temporary guideline along the fold. Unfold and refold the fabric crossways and repeat. Where the two lines meet, this is the centre. The centre of the design should correspond to the centre of the fabric. To find the centre of our design, follow the horizontal and vertical lines indicated by the arrows; the centre is where the lines meet. Start as close to the centre as possible.

WASHING AND PRESSING

The embroidery is machine washable in cold water — on the delicate cycle. Use a mild detergent that contains no bleaching agents. Place between two white sheets and lay flat to dry.

The embroidery should not be dampened and rolled up; instead place it wrong-side up on the top of a soft piece of cloth. Dampen a thin piece of cloth, wring it out thoroughly, place it on top of the embroidery, and press until the cloth is dry. Then press directly on the back of the embroidery until it is completely dry.

The centre of the design, below, should correspond to the centre of the fabric; the arrows will help you (see "How to start" at left).

COLOUR KEY

	DMC	DFT	
• •	745	16	Cream
○○	922	93	Light orange
⊙⊙	946	504	Bright orange
●●	703	101	Bright green
▽▽	909	8	Blue green
▼▼	310	240	Black
△△	726	31	Yellow
▲▲	946	147	Deep green

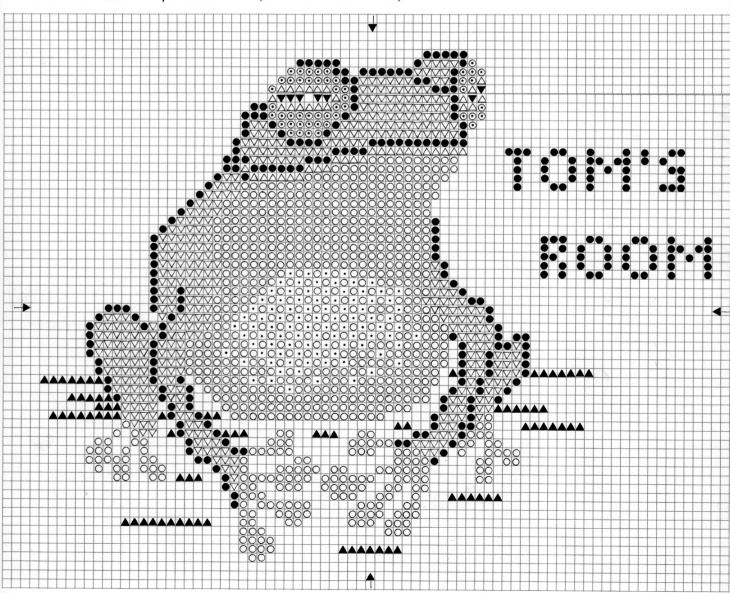

EASY QUILTING

Lithe cats and blithe mice are fun on a quilt and cushion — or make a magpie cushion (great for football fans). They were designed by Margaret Rolfe, and, using her innovative patchwork method, you sew only straight seams while joining pieces in the order numbered.

HOW TO QUILT BY HAND

1. Tack backing, batting and patchwork top together, with no wrinkles in any layer. Tack in a grid with lines 10-15cm apart.
2. Place centre of tacked patchwork on top of inner ring of the quilting hoop, and press outer ring down. The patchwork should be smooth, but not drum tight.
3. With one hand on top and one hand below, begin quilting, using a small running stitch. Start with a knot which should be gently pulled through into the batting layer.
4. Make your stitches as even as possible, and ensure they go through all layers by grazing the pointer finger of the underneath hand with each stitch. Use a thimble to push the needle.
5. End with a small back stitch, and then run thread away into the batting and snip off the remaining thread.
6. Finish quilting the area accessible in the hoop, then move the hoop to an adjacent area. Continue in this manner till the quilting is complete.

Above: the quilt in a hoop; stitches go through all layers. **Right:** cutaway view of the hands at work.

Cat and Mouse Quilt and Cat Cushion

Materials: Sharp HB pencil, ruler, coloured pencils, glue stick, scissors (for paper and fabric), pins, sewing machine, needles (including "between" needle size 8 or 9 for quilting), steam iron, a quilting hoop (about 36cm in diameter).

Template material: Graph paper (sheets A2 or A3 size), cardboard (large sheets medium weight).

HOW TO MAKE THE DESIGNS
Making the templates

1. Draw a square the required size on the graph paper — 24 x 24cm for the cats, 8 x 8cm for the mouse.
2. Copy the designs into the squares, 1 square represents 1cm. Number each shape following the numbers on the design. Indicate the colour for each shape with your coloured pencils.
3. Paste graph paper to cardboard, and cut out all shapes. These shapes are your templates, the master patterns.

Constructing a block

1. Select fabrics according to the colour guide given for each design. Place templates face down on the wrong side of the fabric, and mark around the shape with a sharp pencil. Mark closely around the template so that shapes are not distorted. Leave 2cm between each piece. The line you are marking will be your sewing line. Keep the grain of the fabric going in the same di-rection throughout the block (the same direction as the lines on the graph paper).
2. Cut out pieces, cutting 6mm outside the marked lines to make a 6mm seam allowance.
3. Lay out the pieces of the block in their correct place according to the diagram. Always replace in position after each seam, referring back to the design.
4. Follow the sewing order for each design when joining the pieces together. The numbers re-fer to the number given to each template piece in the design. The sewing order has been designed to be the easiest way of putting the block together so that all the seams are straight sewing. The symbol + means to join pieces together. For instance, 1 + 2 + 3 means to stitch pieces 1, 2 and 3 together, and the unit thus created is called (1-3). If piece 4 is added to this, the instructions continue (1-3) + 4, which creates a unit des-cribed as (1-4). Sometimes you will leave aside a section you have made, and begin work on other pieces which will be joined later. For example, 5 + 6 means leave aside previous sections, and sew only 5 and 6 together to make (5,6). This new section can then be joined to section (1-4), and the in-structions will read (1-4) + (5,6). Follow the instructions step-by-step, like a knitting pattern, and you will have no problems.
5. To sew: pin pieces right sides together, matching the marked lines on wrong sides. Machine stitch along marked lines. Press seams to one side after sewing.

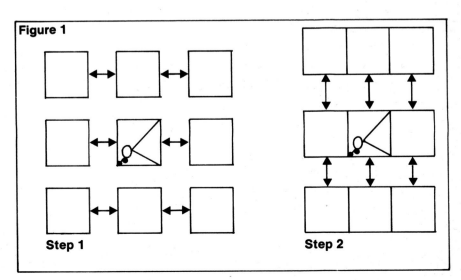

Figure 1

Step 1   **Step 2**

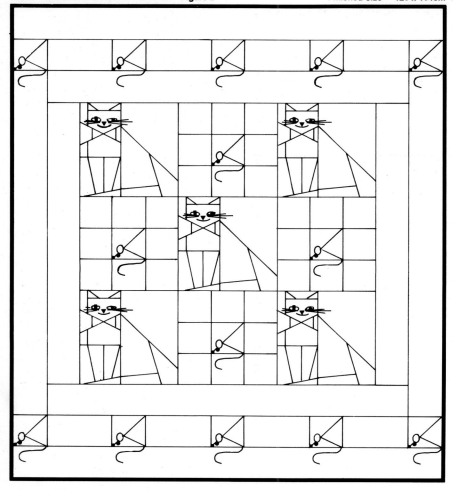

seams. Join the rectangles to mice blocks, making two strips. Join mice strips to the top and bottom of the quilt.

6. From check fabric, mark 2 strips 8cm x 104cm and cut out plus seams. Join to top and bottom of the quilt.

Applique and embroidery

1. Cats' eyes: cut out eye shape from a piece of light cardboard. Cut out eyes from yellow fabric, 6mm larger than cardboard shape. Using a steam iron, press fabric around cardboard shape. Repeat to make 10 eyes. Stitch eyes in place, using thread to match the yellow.
2. Mice's ears: cut out ear shape from light cardboard. Cut out 14 ears from white fabric, and following same procedure as for cats' eyes, cut out, press, and sew in place.
3. Using two strands of embroidery thread and stem stitch, embroider pupils in the eyes, whiskers, mouth, and noses on the cats, and tails and eyes on the mice. Using satin stitch, put noses on the mice.

Constructing the quilt

1. Cut out backing and batting 5cm larger all round then quilt top.

CAT AND MOUSE QUILT AND CAT CUSHION

Materials: fabrics for quilt and cushion (cotton or polycotton fabrics, 114cm wide): 1.50m red (includes fabric for binding and cushion back); 1m white; 1.5m red and white check; scraps of yellow fabric for eyes; backing fabric: white lawn — 2m x 114cm; batting — 2m x 114cm; threads: white thread for machine sewing, yellow thread for applique, quilting thread, skein of black stranded embroidery thread, 30cm zip for back of the cushion.

CAT AND MOUSE QUILT

Constructing the cat and mouse blocks

1. Following the general instructions, the colour guide and sewing order for each design, make 5 sitting cat blocks and 14 mice.
2. Make a template for a square 8 x 8cm. Mark and cut out 16 red check squares and 16 red squares, leaving a 6mm seam allowance around each square. Lay out 4 red, 4 check and 1 mouse square in the pattern given for the blocks between the cat blocks. Stitch the squares together in rows (Figure 1,

step 1), then stitch the rows together to make the block (Figure 1, step 2).

Constructing the quilt top

1. For quilt design, refer to Figure 2, above.
2. Join cat and mouse blocks together, first joining the blocks into rows, then joining the rows to make centre square of quilt.
3. Add first border of red fabric (note — cut out all pieces with 6mm seam allowances around your marked lines):
   1. Mark 2 strips 8cm x 72cm and cut out plus seams. Join to either sides of the cat and mouse square.
   2. Mark 2 strips 8cm x 88cm and cut out plus seams. Join to top and bottom of the cat and mouse square.
4. From check fabric, mark 2 rectangles 8 x 88cm and cut out plus seams. Join to either side of the quilt top.
5. From check fabric, mark 8 rectangles 8 x 16cm and cut out plus

MOUSE

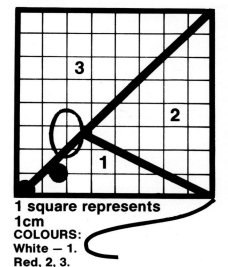

1 square represents 1cm
COLOURS:
White — 1.
Red, 2, 3.

SEWING ORDER:
1. 1 + 2
2. (1, 2) + 3

SITTING CAT 1 square represents 1cm

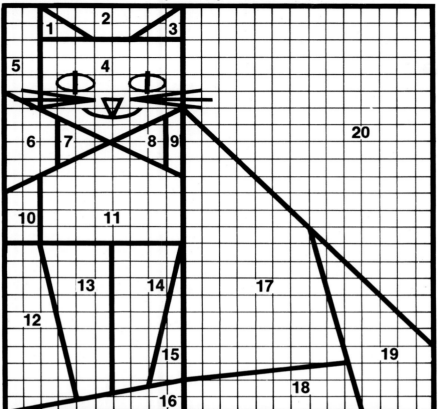

2. Lay backing fabric down on a smooth surface, right side down. Lay batting on top of backing.

3. Spread quilt top over batting, right side up.

4. Pin layers together. Tack quilt in a grid, making lines 10-15cm apart. Remove pins. Make sure there are no wrinkles in the layers.

5. Place quilt in hoop, and quilt around the cats, mice and other shapes. Begin quilting in the centre, then work towards outside.

7. Trim away excess batting and backing at the edges, and remove tacking.

8. From red fabric, cut strips 8cm wide on the bias. Join strips together to make length 4.5m long. Press in half lengthwise.

9. Pin bias strip to the edge of the quilt on the right side, matching the raw edge of the quilt with the raw edges of the folded bias strip. Round the corners slightly, and overlap neatly where the ends of the strip meet. Machine bias strip in place.

10. Fold bias strip to the back of the quilt and hand stitch in place.

COLOURS:
White — 1, 3, 4, 9, 11, 13, 14, 15, 16, 17, 18.
Red — 7, 8.
Red check — 2, 5, 6, 10, 12, 19, 20.

SEWING ORDER:
1. 1 + 2 + 3
2. (1-3) + 4
3. (1-4) + 5
4. 6 + 7
5. (1-5) + (6, 7)
6. 8 + 9
7. 10 + 11
8. (8, 9) + (10, 11)
9. (1-7) + (8-11)
10. 12 + 13 + 14 + 15
11. (12-15) + 16
12. (1-11) + (12-16)
13. 17 + 18
14. (17, 18) + 19
15. (17-19) + 20
16. (1-16) + (17-20)

CAT CUSHION WITH FRILLS
Constructing the cushion top

1. Following the general instructions, the colour guide and sewing order given, make block of crouching cat.

2. Make borders: from red fabric, cut 4 strips 8cm wide and approximately 40cm long, and add to the sides and top and bottom of the block. (Note — the 8cm width includes seam allowances.)

3. Following instructions as for quilt, applique and embroider eyes, nose, and whiskers.

Constructing the cushion

1. Cut out square of white lawn as backing fabric for the quilting, 5cm larger all around than cushion top.

2. Cut out batting same size as backing fabric.

3. Lay backing fabric down, smooth batting over it, and put cat block on top, right side up. Make sure all layers are smooth. Pin layers together, then tack in a grid of lines 10cm apart. Remove pins.

4. Place in hoop, and quilt around cat.

5. Using a wide zigzag stitch, sew around the outside of the cushion top, rounding the corners as you go. Trim away excess backing and batting, remove tacking.

6. Make back of cushion: cut a square of red fabric the width of the cushion top plus 5cm in length. Cut in half through longer sides. Insert zip, using extra length to make seam allowances around the zip.

7. Making the frills:

1) Cut strips of white fabric 14cm wide. Join together to make a strip 140cm long, then join two ends together to make a circle. Neaten seam allowances (or use french seams). Press and machine sew a narrow hem on one edge.

2) Repeat step 1) with check fabric, cutting the strips 8cm wide.

3) Pin the strips with raw edges together, and the check fabric in front of the white fabric. Pin mark into four. On the side of the raw edges, run a gathering stitch between the pin marks, and draw up the gathers.

8. With right side up, place marker pins at the centre of each of the four sides of the cushion. Pin frills to quilted cushion top, right side down, matching pins on frill with marker pins on sides of the cushion. Place raw edges together, and

outside of frill toward the centre of the cushion. Adjust gathers, putting more fullness at the corners.
9. Place back of cushion on top of pinned frills, right side down, pin in place. Stitch around the outside of the cushion. Turn right side out.

COLOURS:
White — 1, 3, 4, 6, 9, 10, 12, 14.
Red check — 5, 7.
Red — 2, 8, 11, 13, 15, 16, 17.

SEWING ORDER:
1. 1 + 2 + 3
2. (1-3) + 4 + 5
3. 6 + 7
4. 8 + 9
5. (1-5) + (6, 7) + (8, 9)
6. 10 + 11 + 12
7. (10-12) + 13 + 14
8. (10-14) + 15
9. (1-9) + (10-15)
10. (1-15) + 16 + 17

CROUCHING CAT   1 square represents 1cm

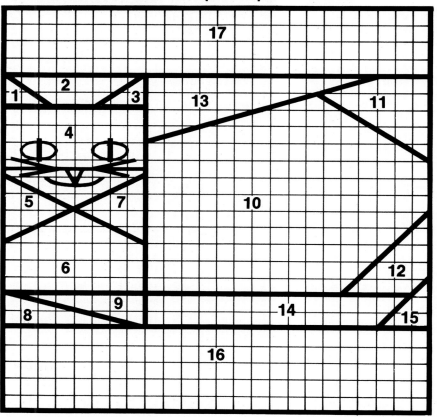

Magpie Cushion

Materials: fabrics — use cotton or polycotton fabrics, 92cm wide: 50cm black for bird, back of cushion and bias binding; 40cm print for background and borders; scraps of white, brown and grey for bird, eye and perch; 50 x 50cm square of polyester batting; 50 x 50cm square of cotton lawn to back quilting; 30cm zip; threads to match fabrics for machine piecing and quilting; black stranded embroidery thread.

For equipment and general instructions on how to make templates and construct the bird block, see directions for Cat and Mouse Quilt and Cushion.

Constructing the cushion top

1. Following the general instructions, the colour guide and sewing order given, make magpie block.
2. Applique eye: cut eye shape from cardboard. Cut circle of brown fabric 6mm larger than cardboard shape. Press fabric circle around cardboard circle, then remove cardboard. Hand stitch in place. Satin stitch a small white highlight on the eye.
3. Using 2 strands of black embroidery thread, chain stitch leg and foot.
4. Make borders: from background fabric, cut 4 strips 8cm wide and approximately 40cm long, and add to the sides and top and bottom of the block. **Note:** 8cm width includes seam allowances.

Constructing the cushion

1. Lay square of lawn backing fabric down, place square of batting over it, and put magpie block on top, right side up. Make sure all layers are smooth. Pin layers together.
2. Machine quilt around magpie, using threads to match fabrics.
3. Using a wide zigzag stitch, sew around the outside of the cushion top, rounding the corners as you go. Trim away excess backing and batting.
4. Make the back of cushion: cut a square of black fabric the width of the cushion top plus 5cm in length. Cut in half through longer sides. Insert zip, using extra length to make seam allowances around the zip.
5. Cut strips of black fabric 4cm wide on the bias. Join together to make 150cm in length.
6. Pin cushion together with right sides outside. Pin bias to the edge of the front, easing the bias around the corners. Neatly fold ends where the bias meets and trim away excess length. Machine stitch around, making a 6mm seam.
7. Turn edge of bias under and hand stitch neatly to the back of the cushion.

> **When making cushions leave zipper open a small amount to make the turning out to the right side easier after sewing cushion top and bottom together.**

MAGPIE   1 square represents 1cm

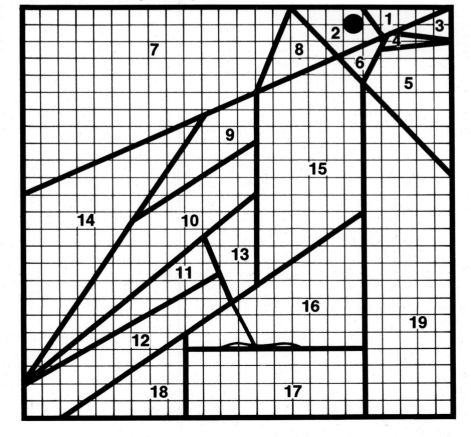

COLOURS:

White — 1, 4, 8, 9, 11.
Black — 2, 6, 10, 13, 15.
Background — 3, 5, 7, 12, 14, 16, 18, 19.
Grey perch — 17.

SEWING ORDER:

1. 1 + 2
2. 3 + 4 + 5
3. (3-5) + 6
4. (1, 2) + (3-6)
5. 7 + 8
6. 9 + 10
7. 11 + 12
8. (11, 12) + 13
9. (9, 10) + (11-13)
10. (9-13) + 14 + 15
11. 16 + 17
12. (16, 17) + 18
13. (9-15) + (16-18)
14. (7, 8) + (9-18) + 19
15. (1-6) + (7-19)

Margaret Rolfe is the author of "Australian Patchwork" (a step-by-step guide to piecing, quilting and applique), published by Lloyd O'Neil and "Quilt a Koala" (Wattle Press).

WINNIE WALLABY

The winsome wallaby was designed for us by Judy Sherman, creator of the Wombat Hollow books in Launceston, Tasmania. Make her cuddly wallaby, as we did, using inside-out sweat shirt fabric. Or substitute fur fabric for longer wear, or strong tweed.

Materials: 70cm x 92cm fabric (tweed, wool, cotton, corduroy or sweat shirt fabric reversed); scrap contrast fabric for ears; a packet of polyester filling (500g); pair of safety eyes; 1 plastic nose (available from most craft shops); fabric glue; pieces of felt for eyelashes, flowers, leaves and paws, plus cape.

1. To make pattern: Draw 5cm squares on paper, copy diagram square by square. Seam allowance is 5mm. Height of wallaby is about 36cm.

2. Cut out fabric using pattern.

3. Press in seam allowance on sides and top of pouch (9). Pin narrow end of pouch to base of front body (2), matching arrows. Machine across.

4. Tack front body and back body (1) together, easing as necessary, leaving neck and base open. Tack base (3) to body, easing as necessary. Machine together. Clip seams.

5. Make ears (6) by machining together ear backs and front contrast pieces. Turn right side out, gather at base.

6. Pin and machine centre face (4) to side face pieces (5), matching X at nose and ● at top of head. Join under jaw X to ■. Tack head back (7) from ● to ●, positioning the ears (inside work), then ● to △. Ease fabric to fit; this gives roundness to the head. Machine together, leaving opening. Turn out. Attach nose. Part fill head, then position eyes. Completely fill head.

7. Fill body firmly. Pin and machine tail (8) from ● to ●. Turn out and fill. Hand sew in position.

8. Attach head to body by hand sewing firmly, placing the pointed part of head back over body at centre back.

9. Hand sew pouch into position, matching ●.

10. Cut paws (11) from felt and sew into position. Cut and fringe eyelashes (14) from felt and glue and sew into position.

To make flowers: cut two petals (12) on fold for each flower. Pinch them together from the back and bind them with thread. Cut green felt leaves (13) and sew leaves and flowers to top of pouch. Sew felt cape (10) around wallaby's shoulders, trim as desired. Sew felt bow on top of head.

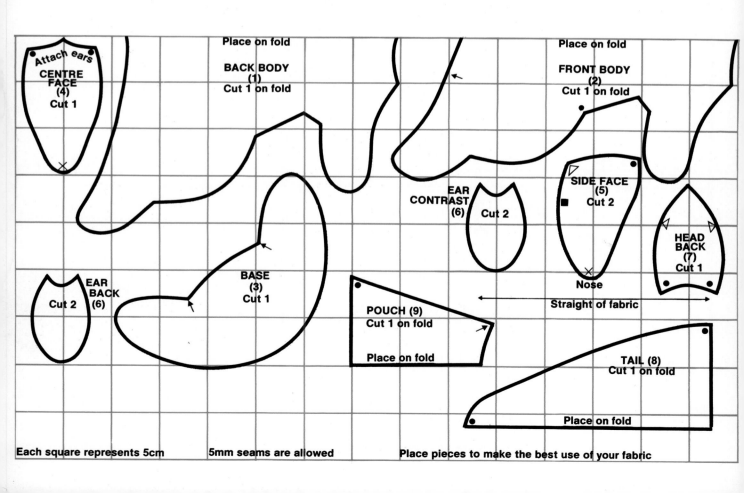

Attach ears
CENTRE FACE (4) Cut 1

Place on fold
BACK BODY (1) Cut 1 on fold

Place on fold
FRONT BODY (2) Cut 1 on fold

EAR CONTRAST (6) Cut 2

SIDE FACE (5) Cut 2

HEAD BACK (7) Cut 1

Nose

Straight of fabric

EAR BACK (6) Cut 2

BASE (3) Cut 1

POUCH (9) Cut 1 on fold

Place on fold

TAIL (8) Cut 1 on fold

Place on fold

Each square represents 5cm   5mm seams are allowed   Place pieces to make the best use of your fabric

CUT THESE PIECES IN FELT

EYELASHES (14)
Cut 2
Fringe
inner
curve

PETALS
(12)
On fold

CAPE (10)
Cut 1 on fold

Place on fold

PAW
(11)
Cut 2

LEAF
(13)
Cut as required

Each square represents 5cm

Papier mâché is a great craft technique, being easy and inexpensive. The only tools and equipment you'll need are in your kitchen. The craft is inexpensive because so many of the materials used — boxes, newspapers, scraps of material — are recycled and once you have mastered the simple techniques, the creative possibilities are endless as Brooke Stanford shows.

We have used one (or in one case, a combination of both) of the following methods:

Torn pieces of newspaper are brushed into place, with a paste, until several layers are built up. The best paste to use is wallpaper paste, bought in powder form. It is most easily mixed in a screw-top jar. Add powder to the water and shake vigorously until thoroughly mixed and smooth.

Paper mash:
1 roll of toilet tissue
4 tablespoons whiting (a thickening element available at hardware stores)
4 tablespoons white synthetic glue
2 tablespoons linseed oil (raw or boiled)
4 tablespoons wallpaper paste (dry)

1. Rip off pieces of the roll of paper and soak in a bucket full of water overnight.

2. Break up the clumps with your hands. Strain the pulp, tapping the strainer to shake out the water.

3. After it is strained, the pulp will form a soft lump, which can be held in your hand. Squeeze out a little more water, but not too much or it will become tough and unworkable.

4. In a bowl, mix in the glue, linseed oil and sprinkle in the dry wallpaper paste, stir again. If the mixture is still too watery, add more wallpaper paste — to take up the extra moisture and make the mash creamier. After applying mash, extra moisture can be soaked up by pressing a tissue onto the mash.

Piggy bank

1. Blow up a balloon. This will form the body.

2. Cover the balloon in several layers of pasted torn newspaper. Allow to dry. The balloon shrinks after the first couple of layers are applied — the wet paste cools down the air in the balloon and it shrinks. Put it in a very low oven for a couple of minutes, keep the door open and watch it, or the balloon will burst as the air heats up inside.

3. Apply a few more layers of pasted newspaper. Allow shape to dry thoroughly.

4. Remove balloon through a small hole cut into pig's face. This will be the snout.

5. Legs and snout were made from kitchen wrap cylinders. Cut cylinders diagonally for the legs, paste into place with strips of newspaper. Paste small cylinder on for snout.

6. Paste pieces of paper over the snout or cover it with a piece of fabric — so money can be retrieved. Leave the legs hollow.

7. Allow pig to dry, sand it, apply a coat of white glue.

8. Cut a slit in pig's back with a scalpel; make it large enough to fit a 50c piece through.

9. Paint the pig, draw on eyes and trotters, allow to dry. Apply several layers of varnish. Add some 'ultra suede' ears, and a tail for effect.

*The same technique was used to produce these two amusing pieces — the piggy bank **below** and the trousers vase **at right**. Directions for trousers on following page.*

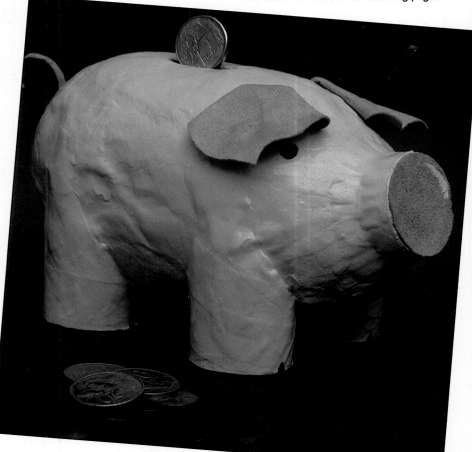

PAPIER
MACHE

Trousers

These were also made with a balloon, but only half the balloon was covered with strips of pasted newspaper. The steps are similar to the piggy bank. Once dry, the rough edges were cut, and the deflated balloon removed. Large postal pack cylinders were used for legs. Newspaper was pasted onto the legs as well. Once dry, a coat of white glue was applied and a thin layer of paper mash smoothed onto the wet glue. It is best to use a knife to do this. The buttoned opening was then moulded. After the mash was dry, another coat of white glue was applied. The patches, hanky, and pocket were dipped in a glue/water mixture (two parts glue to one part water) and stuck in place. Bias binding was given the same treatment, and used to neaten the raw edges of the hem and waist. Another coat of glue was applied. After painting, several coats of varnish were applied.

Remember that a good white synthetic glue (Aquadhere) is very useful as a base for painting. It also seals and toughens.

Tray and coasters

Coasters

1. Cut circles of cardboard to size.

2. Paste layers of newspaper onto both sides of cardboard. Neaten rough edges with strips pasted from front to back.

3. Dry coasters with weights on them to keep them flat.

4. Sand, paint and allow to dry. Apply several coats of varnish to keep coasters water resistant.

Tray

1. The tray was made from two pieces of cardboard. Cut a hemisphere and a long strip about 1.5cm wide.

2. Tape strip to the hemisphere to form the lip of the tray.

3. Cover entire surface, top, bottom and lip with several layers of pasted newspaper.

4. Allow tray to dry, covering it with weights. Avoid marking the work by protecting it with a piece of light cardboard.

5. When dry, paint tray, allow paint to dry. Apply several layers of varnish to keep tray water resistant.

Beads

1. Roll paper mash into balls and thread them carefully onto a piece of wire so they dry with holes in them, ready for threading.

2. When dry, sand them to smooth off rough edges.

3. Paint and varnish beads. When dry, thread beads onto fishing line or strong cotton. We used small plastic beads and a hook and eye fastener to finish off the necklace.

Drying can be hastened in the oven, but prop open the door and don't leave items too long.

The coasters and tray were made from corrugated cardboard from old grocery cartons.

Earrings

1. Flatten paper mash onto a piece of newspaper, using a knife to make it smooth.

2. Allow to dry overnight. When dry, paper mash can be "carved" into desired shape with a scalpel. (You could use a razor blade but be careful of your fingers!)

3. Sand the rough edges of the shape, then glue the pieces together and paint them with a base of white glue.

4. When dry, decorate with bright tempera paints. Apply several coats of varnish.

Fish brooch

The fish was "carved" from dried paper mash, like the earrings, then painted with gold enamel paint. Some of the paint was sanded off, then blue and green tempera paints stippled on with a sponge. A bead was added for an eye along with a piece of tulle, and small plastic beads for scales which were glued on. A brooch pin was glued onto the back. Tail-feathers, bound together with cotton, were glued into a hole made with a pin, after the brooch had been varnished several times and allowed to dry.

The bangle

1. A strip of light cardboard (about 3cm wide) was used as a base. We tried it out for size first, cut it and then taped it, end to end.

2. Paste small pieces of torn newspaper to the inside and outside of the bangle, pasting very narrow pieces from the inside to the outside to neaten the edges.

3. After several layers, dry the bangle on a glass wrapped in newspaper, so that it keeps its shape while drying.

4. When dry, sand surface to make it smooth, then paint with white glue. Decorate with paint and varnish the bangle.

Napkin rings

Made in the same manner as the bangle, we used a cardboard cylinder (kitchen wrap) as a base. One napkin ring was painted with bright tempera paint and varnished, the other was decorated with a bow dipped in a mixture of water and white glue (one part water to two parts glue) which was then glued to the ring. When dry, another coat of white glue was applied before it was painted and varnished. Experiment with different textures; scraps of material, string or lace can all be applied with the water and glue mixture. It is best to give them a coat of straight glue for added strength before painting and varnishing.

Varnishing the finished job is important — to protect it from moisture and damage.

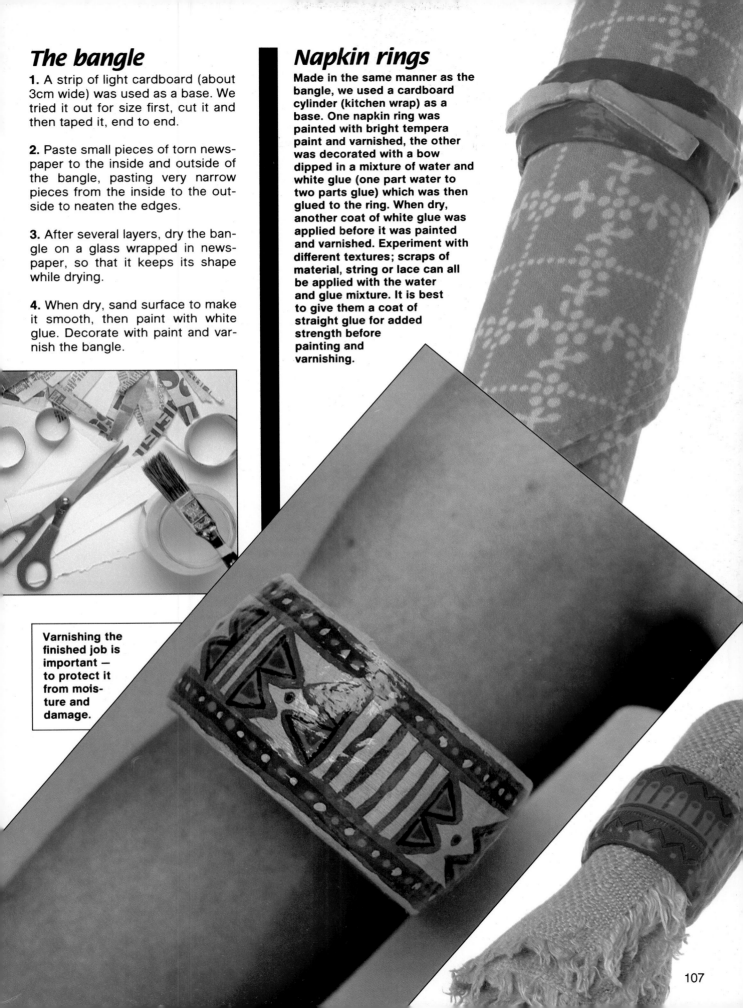

FANTASY FLOWERS

Among the most ingenious ideas we've come across is the transformation of pantihose into fantasy flowers, butterflies and other decorative items! They are easily and inexpensively made using new pantihose mesh stretched firmly over fine wire previously shaped into petals, leaves or butterfly wings. We've even heard of them being used as corsages and bridal bouquets, since they cost little — and last forever. The bright flowers and butterflies here were made by Mrs Margaret Aldham, of Warners Bay, Lake Macquarie, NSW, who suggests that they can be adapted too for serviette rings, table settings, and cake decorations.

At left, delicate butterflies decorated with pearls, glitter and sequins. They can be adapted to decorate gifts, wedding or birthday cakes, serviettes or hair combs. **At right,** some of the intriguing variety of blooms that can be made from pantihose.

1. Make a ring for each petal by winding wire around bottle and twisting off one end. Trim so it won't catch the mesh. Cut stem to required length.

2. Make five rings for single flowers, 10 or 12 rings for double flowers using two ring sizes.

3. Stretch mesh over wire, using straight of material where possible. Hold mesh tightly and tie off with fine wire. Trim excess mesh, press firmly with small pliers.

8. Trim and twist stalks together firmly and bind them neatly with florist's tape.

Materials: New pantihose mesh in colours to suit (old pantihose tends to "run"); very fine wire to No 20 gauge, electric fuse and picture wire (from hardware shops); florist's tape; knitting needles; craft glue (for sticking on stamens and flower centres); scissors; small pliers; assorted bottles; artificial stamens from haberdasher; pearls, beads, buttons, ribbons, glitter; gold and silver thread; fabric dye (if dyeing pantihose to desired shade). There are so many wonderful colours available now that dyeing shouldn't be necessary.

4. Shape petal to suit flower design. Experiment to create different petal shapes.

5. Join petals one at a time, winding fine wire around each extra petal once only.

6. Add stamens or bead centres.

7. When all petals are in place, wind wire around lightly to hold together, then open flowers. Work with one petal overlapping the next until all petals are neat and stamens are secure.

For double flowers, do not tie off until second row of petals has been fixed in the same way as the first. Leaves are made the same way as petals but are bound individually with florist's tape. Veins may be embroidered with silver or gold thread. The same principle applies to butterfly wings. For larger butterflies, pantihose can be wadded together with strong thread bound around them to keep the shape. Fabric paint can be used to create patterns.

To crimp or flute edges of 'petals', use a knitting needle, slim dowling rod, pencil or similar object. First make the ring to the required size, then, using knitting needle, push in gently on outside edge; put needle inside ring and push out; continue the process, turning the ring all the time. For daisy petals, pull out end with the needle, then push V-shape with needle from the outside in.

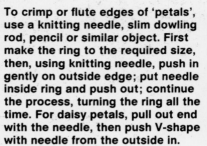

Vibrant colours and an unusual flocked design are the features of the flowers pictured on these pages.

Cook- and Wrap!
GIFTS TO MAKE IN THE KITCHEN

Gifts you make yourself are often the most appreciated. Here are some creations from the kitchen by Jacqui Hing, for Christmas or any other special occasion. Pretty wrapping makes all the difference.

Tartare sauce

1 cup mayonnaise
2 teaspoons chopped capers
1 tablespoon chopped gherkins
1 teaspoon chopped fresh herbs
1 egg, hard-boiled and grated

Combine mayonnaise with capers, gherkins and herbs. Lastly, fold in grated egg.

Spiced quail eggs

24 quail eggs
750 mls white wine vinegar
2 teaspoons black peppercorns
2 teaspoons yellow mustard seeds
2 teaspoons cumin seeds

Place quail eggs in steamer over pan of boiling water, steam for about 8 minutes, cool under running water. Combine vinegar in pan with peppercorn, mustard and cumin seeds. Cover and bring to boil, reduce heat, simmer 15 minutes, strain and cool. Place shelled eggs into sterilized jars. Cover completely with spiced vinegar, seal, keep in refrigerator for up to one month.

Mayonnaise

2 egg yolks
1 teaspoon French mustard
½ teaspoon salt
¼ teaspoon pepper
½ teaspoon lemon juice
1 cup olive oil
2 tablespoons white wine vinegar

Place the yolks, seasonings and lemon juice in a mixing bowl. Whisk or beat at low speed on electric mixer for a minute or so. Add oil, drop by drop, whisking continuously until about ¼ cup of oil has been added. Add 1 to 2 teaspoons of vinegar to thin the mixture down, whisking continuously. More vinegar can be added, depending on the taste and thickness required.

Tomato mayonnaise

1 cup mayonnaise
2 tablespoons cream
1 to 2 tablespoons tomato paste
a little tabasco sauce

Combine ingredients, mix well.

Mango and ginger chutney

8 green mangoes, peeled and diced
2 cups undersize tomatoes, peeled, seeded and chopped
4 cups sliced onions
2 tablespoons finely sliced fresh ginger
2 cups raisins
1 cup sultanas
4 cups brown sugar
3 cups vinegar
¼ cup salt
2 tablespoons curry powder

Mix all the ingredients together in a saucepan, boil for 1 hour. Pour into jar and seal.

Spiced oil

2 cups vegetable oil
6 black peppercorns
6 whole coriander seeds
2 cloves garlic
1 red chilli, finely chopped
2 slices fresh ginger (½ cm)

Crush ginger seeds, peel and bruise garlic. Combine all ingredients. Pour into 2 cup capacity bottle and allow to infuse at least 10 days before use. Store in a cool, dark place.

Herbed vinegar

2 cups white wine vinegar
2 sprigs rosemary
1 stalk tarragon
2 fresh thyme sprigs
1 fresh oregano sprig

Place herbs in a 2 cup capacity bottle. Heat the vinegar, pour hot vinegar in bottle over herbs. Allow to cool, then cap bottles. Leave for 2 weeks to allow flavour to develop. Use as a gift with some olives which can be marinaded in a mixture of the oil and vinegar.

Honey pickled pears

2 cups honey
1 cup cider vinegar
1 cinnamon stick
6 cloves
12 pears, peeled, cored and quartered

Place the honey, vinegar, cinnamon and cloves in a saucepan and bring to boil. Cook the fruit, a third at a time, in the syrup. Move occasionally, let them simmer until they are transparent. Drain and place in sterilised storage jars. Cover with the syrup and seal.

From left: Tomato mayonnaise; Mayonnaise; Tartare sauce; Herbed vinegar; Spiced oil; Spiced quail eggs; Mango and ginger chutney; Honey pickled pears.

Glassware is Bodum from Vasa Agencies, Sydney.

Lemon almond crescents

1¼ cups plain flour
2 tablespoons castor sugar
125g butter
⅓ cup ground almonds
2 teaspoons grated lemon rind
1 egg yolk
1 tablespoon water approx
½ cup icing sugar

Sift flour in a bowl, stir in sugar. Rub in the butter, stir in ground almonds and lemon rind. Add the egg yolk and enough water to mix to a soft dough. Roll walnut-sized pieces of dough into 5 cm lengths, then shape into crescents. Place onto greased oven trays, bake in a moderate oven for 12 minutes or until pale brown. Cool on wire rack, sift on icing sugar while warm.

Makes about 30.

Passionfruit and lemon butter

1 lemon, juice and grated rind
4 passionfruit
125g butter
2 cups sugar
4 egg yolks, beaten together

Place the juice, grated rind, passionfruit pulp, butter and sugar in top of double saucepan, or in a bowl over a pan of boiling water. Stir until sugar is dissolved. Add the egg yolks, stirring continuously until mixture thickens. Pour into hot jars. Cover lightly and seal when cool. Give as a gift with individual tartlet cases.

Mini plum puddings

1 kg mixed dried fruit
3 eggs
1 cup brown sugar, firmly packed
300 ml carton cream
2¼ cups plain flour
2 tablespoons brandy

Beat eggs and sugar in the small bowl of electric mixer until thick and creamy. Add cream and beat until combined. Place mixed fruit into large bowl, stir in egg mixture, then flour and brandy. Spoon mixture into 3-4 small greased pudding basins, cover with lid or grease-proof paper and foil. Steam in a large pan of boiling water (making sure the water level only comes half-way up the sides of pudding basin) for 3 hours. Steam a further 1 hour to reheat on day of serving. Make 2 weeks ahead. Give it away in a pudding dish wrapped in a checked cloth, tied on top with a bright ribbon.

Right: back, from left: Raspberry Cointreau icecream sauce; Lollipops; **centre, from left:** *Liqueur creme fraiche; Chocolate-dipped strawberries;* **front:** *Swirled chocolates.* **Below: back, from left:** *Mini plum pudding; Passionfruit and lemon butter;* **front:** *Lemon almond crescents.*

Background paper, cards, boxes from R. J. Phillips, Sydney; creme fraiche bowl from Kosta Boda, Sydney.

Lollipops

1 cup sugar
½ cup water
food colouring
bamboo skewers

Combine sugar and water in pan. Stir over heat without boiling until sugar is dissolved. Bring to boil, boil without stirring until mixture is golden brown. Remove from heat.

Pour half the mixture into a heatproof container. Colour each mixture with a few drops of food colouring by blending in lightly with a fork; do not stir or the mixture might crystallize.

Spoon small amounts of mixture onto an oiled tray. Press skewers into centre of each one. Allow to cool on tray.

Makes approx. 12.

Variations: Hundreds and thousands, coconut and other toppings can be sprinkled onto toffee circles before they set.

Raspberry Cointreau icecream sauce

500g fresh or frozen raspberries
⅓ cup castor sugar
1 tablespoon lime juice
2 tablespoons Cointreau

Thaw raspberries, reserve juice, blend or process raspberries, juice, sugar, lime juice, Cointreau until smooth. Push through sieve to remove seeds. Store in refrigerator for up to two weeks.

Swirled chocolates

200g block white chocolate
200g milk chocolate
200g dark chocolate
food colourings
flavourings
chocolate moulds

Melt the chocolate separately in a heatproof bowl or double saucepan over gently simmering water, stir until melted, or microwave on Low for 3-4 minutes.

To mould: spoon chocolate into dry, clear moulds. Refrigerate until set. Remould chocolate, store in airtight container. To swirl: spoon a little of the chocolate, using two colours, into moulds until full. Swirl lightly with a skewer to achieve desired effect. Refrigerate until set.

Variations: add a few drops of food colouring to the melted white chocolate. Flavouring, such as rum or peppermint essence, can be added to the chocolates.

Liqueur creme fraiche

¾ cup thickened cream
¾ cup sour cream
¼ cup castor sugar
1 teaspoon vanilla essence
1 tablespoon Grand Marnier

Combine cream and sour cream. Cover, leave unrefrigerated until thick (2-3 days). Stir in sugar, essence and Grand Marnier. Refrigerate up to 1 week. Present the creme fraiche with a basket of succulent fresh fruit.

Chocolate-dipped strawberries

125g dark chocolate
2 x 250g punnets strawberries

Melt chocolate in bowl over pan of hot water. Holding onto strawberry stem, dip half of strawberry into chocolate, remove, allowing excess to run off. Place onto foil-covered tray, refrigerate until set.

Spicy cheese biscuits

125g butter
2 egg yolks
1 cup grated tasty cheese
2 cups plain flour
4 tablespoons sesame seeds
1 tablespoon poppy seeds
1½ teaspoons dried mustard
1½ teaspoons paprika

Beat butter and egg yolks in small bowl with electric mixer until light and fluffy. Add cheese and flour, beat on low speed until just combined. Knead mixture on lightly floured board until smooth, roll out thinly. Cut into rounds using a 4cm fluted cutter, place rounds onto greased oven trays. Brush each one lightly with beaten egg white, sprinkle with combined sesame seeds, poppy seeds, mustard and paprika. Bake in moderately hot oven (200°C) for about 12 minutes, cool on wire rack. Store biscuits in airtight container.

Makes approximately 50.

Below: back, from left: gift basket of ribbon pasta, Tomato sauce supreme and fresh mushrooms; Spicy Christmas mix; front, from left: Fruity cheese roll; Spicy cheese biscuits. Right: Mini cheese dampers. Butters, from left: Herbed garlic butter, Mustard butter.

Tomato sauce supreme

2 tablespoons olive oil
2 onions, chopped
2 cloves garlic, crushed
1 hot chilli (optional)
2 bacon rashers, chopped
2 large ripe tomatoes, peeled, chopped
½ cup red wine
2 tablespoons fruit chutney
375g sliced mushrooms
¼ cup chopped fresh basil

Heat oil, saute onions, garlic, chilli and bacon until onions have softened. Add tomatoes, wine and chutney, bring to the boil, reduce heat and simmer with lid off for 30 minutes or until tomatoes are very pulpy and mixture has reduced by about a third. Cool.

To serve, reheat sauce in a pan, add 375g sliced mushrooms and fresh basil, simmer 5 minutes, spoon over cooked pasta. Place sauce in a jar and give away in a basket with fresh mushrooms, a bunch of basil, pasta and a bottle of red wine!

Tomato sauce, pasta storage jars from Davmac, Sydney; wooden boards from Peter Sorensen Woodware, Sydney; butter dishes from R. J. Phillips, Sydney.

Mini cheese dampers

4 cups self-raising flour
2½ cups buttermilk
1 tablespoon fresh or 1 teaspoon dried basil leaves
1 tablespoon fresh or 1 teaspoon dried oregano leaves
2 teaspoons dried mustard
2 teaspoons paprika
1 cup grated tasty cheese
1 tablespoon sesame seeds

Place flour in a mixing bowl. Add enough buttermilk to give a soft, slightly sticky dough. Divide mixture in half. In one half, knead in basil and oregano. In the other half, knead in the mustard and paprika until combined and smooth. Shape each dough into a round, place on greased oven trays, pat out to about 5cm thick. Using a sharp knife, mark each one into 8 wedges and cut about 1cm deep. Sprinkle each round with cheese and sesame seeds. Bake in a hot oven (220°C) for about 10 minutes. Reduce heat to moderately hot (180°C), bake a further 15 minutes or until golden brown. Damper should sound hollow when the base is tapped. Alternatively, dough can be frozen, wrapped and given away with instructions on how to bake.

Spicy Christmas mix

1 cup smoked almonds
1 cup cashews
1 cup Japanese rice crackers
1 cup pretzel knots
¼ cup oil
2 teaspoons Worcestershire sauce
2 teaspoons curry powder
½ teaspoon cayenne pepper

Combine all ingredients, spread out onto oven tray. Bake in moderately slow oven (150°C) for 15 minutes, being careful not to brown too much. Stir occasionally. Cool on tray.

Store in an airtight container.

Fruity cheese roll

250g pkt cream cheese
¼ cup sultanas
¼ cup chopped dried apricots
¼ cup chopped glace pineapple
1 tablespoon mixed peel
2 tablespoons sweet sherry
½ cup grated tasty cheese
1 teaspoon grated lemon rind
¾ cup poppy seeds

Combine fruit and sherry in a bowl, stand 2 hours. Beat cream cheese and tasty cheese in a small bowl with electric mixer until smooth. Stir in lemon rind and fruits, refrigerate until firm. Roll mixture into a log shape, about 20 cm long. Roll in poppy seeds, cover, store in refrigerator for up to 4 days.

Mustard butter

125g butter, softened
1 tablespoon seeded mustard
2 teaspoons, lime juice

Cream butter, add mustard and lime juice and beat until well combined. Place into ramekins and refrigerate to store.

Herbed garlic butter

125g butter
1 tablespoon chopped parsley
2 cloves garlic, crushed
1 tablespoon chopped basil
1 shallot, finely chopped

Cream butter until smooth and creamy. Add remaining ingredients and beat until well combined. Place in ramekins and refrigerate to store. Give butters away with dampers in a pretty basket.

Christmas Countdown
PLAN FOR FUN

For some of us, Christmas is a time of confused last-minute activity; for others, events are planned carefully so that everyone can enjoy the anticipation. Paula Goodyer starts the countdown six weeks in advance . . .

October Alert

Sending gifts and cards to friends in faraway places? Start packing them now. In October, Christmas might seem a long way off to you, but not to Australia Post. Final posting dates for some countries close in early October.

Six weeks to go

• Get your Christmas ideas down on paper. Earmark a note-book for jotting down a Christmas card list, gift list and guest list.

• Add your food plan for the holiday season. What special meals or celebrations are you catering for — a party, a candle-lit Christmas Eve dinner, a light and festive Christmas breakfast, Christmas dinner? Browse through your favourite recipes for ideas and draw up shopping lists of what you need.

• Fancy a big bash but don't have the time? Take advantage of our Christmas climate and pick a favourite beach or picnic spot as the venue — invite all your friends to B.Y.O. festive food and drink.

• Making your own (non-perishable) presents? Get cracking now.

• Contact a favourite charity for their Christmas mail-order catalogue — often a good way of buying inexpensive Christmas cards and stocking fillers with minimum fuss.

• Buy the Christmas turkey now if there's room in your freezer.

• Why not invest in a potted Christmas tree now to avoid a last-minute rush (and inflated prices). Norfolk pines make a good symmetrical shape for decorating — keep in a sunny spot and water well.

*Christmas decorations needn't be expensive — the splendour of the arrangement **at right** depends mainly upon ivy, woven into a garland, a traditional tree, red satin ribbons and pine cones. Show originality by decorating gifts with dried Australiana, **as above**, including various leaves.*

Five weeks to go

• Avoid a last-minute supermarket marathon and buy non-perishables, including ingredients for baking. Now's a good time to seize almond paste, jars of mincemeat and cranberry sauce — vital items that disappear from supermarket shelves closer to Christmas.

• Buy (or start making your own) Christmas cards. Buy stamps.

• Be on the lookout for Christmas gifts now. Fetes are good sources for homemade treats and unusual handcrafts.

• December gets booked out fast, so do any necessary inviting now. Tot up the numbers and check if you have enough glasses, cutlery, crockery, chairs. Arrange to borrow or buy extras. Consider saving money (and energy) with disposable plates and cups — a good idea for small children.

• Think about a table setting. If you have time, you could make your own tablecloth, napkins or placemats in some of the festive fabrics available now (how about some extras for giving?). Too busy? File away this simple idea for a (cool) white Christmas — a lacy white cloth with a centrepiece of white roses or daisies, white wine, crisp doilies, white frosted cake . . .

• Buy (or make) advent calendars for the kids, so they can begin opening presents on December 1.

Above, simplest of all table decorations: candle and dried dollar gum leaves sprayed silver. **Below**, make individual greeting cards with simple drawings and paste-and-cut method. Designs, simple or complicated, can be achieved by sticking coloured paper onto cardboard in layers and then cutting out shapes carefully with scalpel or cutting knife. Different colours are revealed with each shape that is cut and removed. Our artist used brown paper for one layer.

Four weeks to go

• Missed surface mail to friends overseas? Airmail deadlines are now breathing down your neck — earliest closing dates are around the second week of December. Last minute lightweight gifts include: Australiana (of the gum leaves and gum nut variety) in Christmas decorations and jewellery, Australian teas, Australian paperbacks and T-shirts, magazine subscriptions, lingerie. For children: marsupial glove puppets, May Gibbs' posters or friezes, kites, appliqued bibs.

• Start shopping for local gifts in earnest. Don't forget ribbon, gift wrap, adhesive tape and glue.

• No room to hide bulky presents? Ask a neighbour to gift-sit.

• Make your cake and pud. Fast alternative: buy them now and drizzle them with rum and/or brandy for extra richness come Christmas.

• Taking the kids to a Christmas show or panto? Book seats now.

Above: make unusual, inexpensive tree ornaments by gluing together a selection of pasta shapes and spray painting them. To make the flower-like shape, for example, glue the first lot of pasta shells onto a round piece of cardboard then glue other shells to bottom layer. Spray paint. To make tinsel wreath, **left**, make a wire coathanger into a round shape. Straighten hook and wrap around wire. Secure beginning of tinsel to wire with tape or thin wire and continue wrapping around until it is as thick as you wish. Tie a ribbon at base or top, hang on a hook.

MERRY CHRISTMAS

One week to go

• Aim to plan this week so you can *enjoy* Christmas Eve instead of spending it in a lather of cleaning, cooking and gift-wrapping.

• Buy a tree and decorate it. Or save with a cheap alternative. A bush walk will yield a dead branch you can spray white and decorate with anything you fancy (coloured hearts, or red and green bows).

• Keep the children busy decorating the house and making a Christmas wreath for the door.

• Going away for the holidays? Cancel the milk and papers.

• Do remaining shopping. If you still have presents to find, here are some quick (and thoughtful) gifts you can shop for in the supermarket or delicatessen: a small wooden cheeseboard piled with boxed cheeses and pumpernickel; a pretty giftbag filled with chocolates, chocolate biscuits (perhaps a chocolate lovers' cookbook too?). Or pack inexpensive gift baskets with any of these good-for-you treats like exotic fruits and macadamias; a selection of delicatessen goodies; an assortment of quality teas and biscuits.

• Pick up the turkey and ham — don't forget a frozen turkey can take two to three days to thaw out in the fridge.

• Ice and/or decorate your cake. Short of time? Miss out the layer of almond paste under the icing and flavour the frosting with almond essence instead.

• If you don't want children to know which present is which under the tree, label the gifts with numbers.

• Make sure you have more than enough ice cubes — freeze extra for the thirsty hordes.

Two weeks to go

• School holidays are close. Plan to keep boredom at bay with Christmas projects like: gathering dried foliage and grasses for a wreath; making traditional baked dough decorations studded with red and green angelica; cutting out simple shapes using red or green card and cookie cutters (like hearts, stars and gingerbread men) for hanging on the tree and tagging presents; making their own bonbons (from lunchwrap tubes and crepe paper) filled with do-it-yourself paper hats and bad jokes; card plus a packet of stars and glitter will keep them busy making Christmas cards.

• Check the drinks supply. Do you have enough mixers and fruit juices? Why not plan a special cocktail or two, including the non-alcohol kind.

• Do you need emergency nibbles (nuts, biscuits, canned delicacies) for unexpected visitors?

• Make sure you have enough film for your camera.

• Make any freezable dishes for parties or Christmas Day.

• Check the cutlery, china and tablecloth you plan to use and see if anything needs cleaning.

• Schedule a family houseblitz — one or two hours in which *the whole family* (not just you) cleans and tidies. Make a thorough job of it so that only minimal cleaning will need to be done in the last week.

Three weeks to go

• Order your Christmas turkey and ham, for the best prices.

• Arrange appointments if you need a haircut, manicure or facial.

• Treat yourself to a dazzling new party outfit.

• Dust off the Christmas decorations. Do you need to buy more? Do the tree lights still work?

• Going away for Christmas? Ask a neighbour to collect mail, water plants and keep a watchful eye on your house.

• Schedule a day for making your own handmade originals — do-it-yourself presents like your own handsomely decanted herb vinegar, Christmas cookies, brandied fruits, shortbread — anything which can be kept or which you can freeze until Christmas. (Don't forget a few extras for emergency gifts.) Even if you're juggling a job and children, a creative session in the kitchen can be a soothing (and inexpensive) alternative to a frantic Saturday shopping with children. See page 114 for ideas.

To make wonderful Christmas balls utilise plain polystyrene balls and transform them with long pins, sequins and beads or pieces of coloured fabric. For the baubles **far left** and **centre left,** thread a bead and a sequin onto a long pin and stick pin into polystyrene ball. Cover entire ball in this way. Add more sequins or beads to a pin for a more complex design. For a completely different effect, use bright scraps of fabric to make ornaments. One way is to cut fabric into small squares and, using a nail file, push fabric into the polystyrene ball. Cover all over in this way. Alternatively, divide ball into four sections by making a shallow cut in surface. Push fabric into the cut with a nail file. Trim edges and push in further to neaten them. Push lace into the cut with the nail file.

Primitive or naive shapes make delightful Christmas decorations. For the angel, **right**, draw the outline onto a piece of corrugated cardboard. Cut out the shape with a scalpel or cutting knife. Paint on features. Glue a skewer or straw onto back of angel — the straw enables the angel to sit on the tree.

Ivy wreath, **left**, makes a no-cost, very effective decoration. Thoughtful, personalised gifts may include seasonal fruit in a basket.

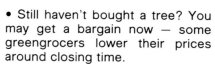

⭐ Christmas eve

• Quick, before the shops shut — have you got everything you need?

• Still haven't bought a tree? You may get a bargain now — some greengrocers lower their prices around closing time.

• Stuff your turkey (cook it if you intend eating it cold); finish any Christmas food preparations.

• Put any remaining gifts under the Christmas tree.

• Put out Santa's favourite tipple with a piece of cake, plus water and carrots for the reindeer — don't forget to make them "disappear" before the kids wake up.

• Play Santa.

• Relax.

Below, everyone loves champagne for special occasions — add a bunch of pretty flowers for a personal touch. Or put colourful jelly beans in a useful jar and decorate with ribbons, **right**.

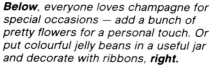

Below, potpourri gifts are always appreciated and even more so if you've made them yourself. See page 20 for details on how to dry the flowers. Clear boxes are available from florists' suppliers.

𝓘ndex

Christmas
— cards 122
— countdown 120
— decorating gifts 120
— fruit in a basket 126
— potpourri gifts 126
— tree ornaments 123, 125
— wreaths 123, 126

Decoupage
— decorative plates 68, 69
— door finger plate 69
— door handles 64
— earrings 64
— lampshade 68
— lampstand 68
— side table 70
— spectacle lenses 68
— wooden box 66

Entertaining
— afternoon teas 10
— atmosphere 10
— barbecues 9
— breakfast parties 6
— brunch parties 6
— buffets 6
— Christmas in June 7
— cocktail parties 4
— cook-ahead ideas 6
— delegating 11
— dinner parties 5
— hostessing 10
— kitchen sense 8
— picnics 9
— novelty parties 7
— quantities 8
— St Patrick's Day 7
— time-saving tips 8

Fantasy flowers 108

Flowers
— basket 19
— cone 15
— containers 16
— hydrangea cone 22
— natives 21
— potpourri 20
— spiced wreath 22
— topiary 24
— top tables 18

Folk Art cat 89

Food
— chocolate-dipped strawberries 117
— edible 'jewellery' 51
— fruity cheese roll 119
— herbed garlic butter 119
— herbed vinegar 115
— honey pickled pears 115
— lemon almond crescents 116
— liqueur creme fraiche 117
— lollipops 116
— mango and ginger chutney 115
— mayonnaise 114
— mini cheese dampers 118
— mini plum puddings 116
— mustard butter 119
— novelty cake 50
— passionfruit and lemon butter 116
— raspberry cointreau icecream sauce 116
— spiced oil 115
— spiced quail eggs 114
— spicy cheese biscuits 118
— spicy Chistmas mix 119
— swirled chocolates 116
— tartare sauce 114
— tomato mayonaise 114
— tomato sauce supreme 118

Gardening
— balcony gardens 55
— drainage 63
— fertilising 60
— indoor plants 53
— money savers 57
— mulching 62
— other tips 63
— pests 61
— pet deterrent 56
— plant diplomacy 55
— plant shelters 62
— sprays 62
— topiary 57
— time savers 58
— when-to-plant guide 60

Kids
— child care 32
— clothes 30
— food 28
— furniture 30
— health and safety 31
— help 32
— immunization 31
— medical records 31
— money 28
— paper art 29
— safety kit 28
— party giving 32
— toiletries 31
— top 10 rules 28
— toys 30
— work or not? 31

Money
— budget checklist 36
— buying a house 40
— credit cards do's and don'ts 39
— disability insurance 42
— getting your house in order 36
— his and her bank accounts 41
— investment portfolio 34
— life insurance 43
— making a will 42
— planning your goals 34
— real estate investment 41
— spending overseas (shopping strategies) 43
— superannuation 42
— weekly budget guide 37

Money savers
— babysitting co-operatives 46
— buying secondhand 44
— dress-up box 45
— food co-operatives 46
— make-up box 46
— recycling your own wardrobe 44
— save on household cleaners 46
— share-a-gadget 46
— useful box 44

Money Spinners
— garage sale 50
— handpaint a garment 47
— homemade food 47
— novelty cakes: dinosaur, edible "jewellery" 50, 51
— services you can provide 48, 50

Paint finishes
— antiquing medium 77
— chamois 76
— crackle 78
— japan paint 76
— negative striping 75
— scumbling medium 76
— spatter 74
— spatter brush 74
— sponging 77
— stipple 77
— strié 77
— terracotta pots 73
— tracing images 78

Pantry planner 12

Papier mâché
— bangle 107
— beads 105
— coasters 104
— earrings 106
— fish brooch 106
— napkin rings 107
— piggy bank 102
— tray 104
— trousers 104

Stencilling
— Bronze powder 82
— paper 82

Things to make
— cat cushion 95
— cat quilt 95
— cross-stitch frog 91
— magpie cushion 99
— wallaby 100

Topiary
— dried 24
— live 57

Recipes

WHITE CHOCOLATE CASES WITH ICECREAM AND APRICOT SAUCE, page 3

Foil pie trays can be bought from kitchenware stores. Chocolate cases will keep, covered, in refrigerator for about a month. Apricot Sauce can be made up to four days ahead. We used commercially made icecream in this recipe.

250g white chocolate, melted
APRICOT SAUCE
½ cup chopped dried apricots
1 cup water
2 tablespoons sugar
¼ teaspoons sugar
¼ teaspoon cinnamon

Using a teaspoon, spread chocolate evenly over base and sides of 4 individual foil pie trays (base measures 7cm); make top edge as even as possible; refrigerate until set. Carefully pull foil trays away from chocolate, serve icecream in chocolate cases, topped with Sauce, fruit and a little extra grated white chocolate if desired.
Apricot Sauce: Combine all ingredients in pan, bring to the boil, reduce heat, simmer, covered, 5 minutes or until apricots have softened (or microwave on High about 4 minutes), cool; blend or process until sauce is smooth.

Serves 4.

Recipe from The Australian Women's Weekly Light and Luscious Summertime Cookbook.

SOLOMON BLUE, page 4

Pour one nip of Bacardi gently into a glass containing ice and having a lemon sugared rim. Follow with a nip of Blue Curacao. Add a frangipanni for decoration. Photo courtesy of Mode magazine.

CREAMY BANANA COLADA, page 3

This rich creamy cocktail is substantial enough to have for lunch by the pool or beach. Make sure coconut milk and pineapple juice are icy cold.

340ml can coconut milk
1½ cups canned pineapple juice
2 ripe bananas, chopped
½ cup white rum

Blend or process coconut milk, pineapple juice, bananas and rum until smooth and creamy. Pour into glasses, decorate with pineapple and toasted coconut, if desired.

Makes about 1 litre.

Recipes from The Australian Women's Weekly Easy Entertaining Cookbook.

CASSIS CHAMPAGNE COCKTAIL, page 3

Cassis is blackcurrant-flavored and Framboise raspberry-flavored.

Cassis or Framboise liqueur
750ml bottle champagne
8 sugar cubes

Place one sugar cube in each of 8 glasses, add a capful or 2 teaspoons of liqueur to each glass. Fill each glass with well chilled champagne, serve immediately.

Serves 6 to 8.

STRAWBERRY AND PASSIONFRUIT ICECREAM VICTORIA, page 3

You will need to use about six large passionfruit for this recipe.

2 x 250g punnets strawberries
2 tablespoons icing sugar
½ cup passionfruit pulp
STRAWBERRY AND PASSIONFRUIT ICECREAM
3 egg yolks
¾ cup castor sugar
1 cup milk
250g punnet strawberries
¼ cup passionfruit pulp
2 x 300ml thickened cream
red food coloring

Halve strawberries. Add icing sugar and passionfruit, serve with icecream.
Strawberry and Passionfruit Icecream: Beat egg yolks and sugar in small bowl with electric mixer until thick and creamy. Heat milk in pan until just below boiling point, reduce heat, gradually stir in egg yolk mixture, stir over low heat, without boiling, until mixture thickens slightly; cool to room temperature. Divide between 2 bowls.

Blend or process strawberries until smooth; you will need ⅔ cup puree for this recipe. Add strawberry puree and 1 carton of cream to 1 bowl of custard; tint pink with a little coloring. Stir passionfruit and remaining carton of cream into remaining custard; mix well. Fold the 2 mixtures together to give a marbled effect. Pour into freezer trays or cake tin, cover with foil, freeze overnight.

Serves 6.

Recipe from The Australian Women's Weekly Light and Luscious Summertime Cookbook.

Acknowledgements:

Photographs by Andrew Payne, Andre Martin, Warwick Kent, Russell Brookes, Jean-Paul Ferrero, Neville Waller, Ern McQuillan, Ashley Mackevicius.

Découpage table, page 71, by Belinda Hemphill; masks, page 26, from Clem, Paddington, NSW; toys, page 30, from Johnson & Johnson; illustrations by Lee McKay; diagrams by Enrico Giammetta; montages by Sabine Pick.

STOCKISTS
Paint supplies: Australia: *Screws Hardware, 118 Queen St, Woollahra, NSW; or The Painted Finish, 2 Paddington St, Paddington, NSW. Enquiries to Dulux Customer Services Department in all states or your local Paint & Paper store.*
New Zealand: *Mac Lesieter, GPO Box 1669, Christchurch.*

EDITOR
Sue Wendt

ART DIRECTOR
Robbylee Phelan

PRODUCTION EDITOR
Maryanne Blacker

ACP EDITOR-IN-CHIEF
Richard Walsh

ACP DEPUTY EDITOR-IN-CHIEF
Dawn Swain

Produced by The Australian Women's Weekly Special Projects Division.
Typeset by Photoset Computer Service Pty Ltd., Sydney, Australia
Printed by Dai Nippon Co Ltd, Tokyo, Japan
Published by Australian Consolidated Press, 54 Park Street, Sydney
Distributed by Network Distribution Company, 54 Park Street, Sydney

Bumper book of bright ideas.

Includes index.
ISBN 0 949128 11 2.

1. Handicraft. 2. Entertaining. 3. Gardening. I. Wendt, Sue. II. Australian Women's Weekly.

745.5